T0090490

ENDORSEMENTS FOR *SUSTAINED*

"If you need upliftment, encouragement, and perseverance, this gem of a book will remind you that you are deeply loved and cared for, and you have all the strength and spiritual resources you need to carry on with dignity, integrity, and grace."

—**Alan Cohen**, Holistic Health Coach and Author of 24 popular inspirational book, including *The Mystical Messiah* and *A Course in Miracles Made Easy*; contributing writer for the #1 New York Times best-selling series *Chicken Soup for the Soul*

"When people lose a loved one, a spouse, friend, daughter or son, it is just awful and painful. When this loss happened to a respected pediatrician, Dr. Peter Nieman, he was able to turn his pain into a teachable moment with love, wisdom and compassion. A must read!"

—**Kyle Yesuda, MD**, former President of the American Academy of Pediatrics

"In a most compassionate and vulnerable manner, Peter Nieman shares valuable life lessons experienced while in the midst of his healing journey. He has a remarkable ability to integrate his knowledge as a physician with the wisdom that can emerge through tragedy. This book will make you stop and reflect deeply on what truly matters and what it means to be human. I was genuinely moved by his insights and his humanity."

—**David Irvine,** author of *Caring Is Everything: Getting to the Heart of Humanity, Leadership, and Life*

"This book is a heartfelt documentary tribute to Ben. It is a riveting, heart wrenching account of your family's journey through what must have been a most traumatic loss. You continue to amaze me with the courage and heart. It is a forever meaningful reading experience."

—**John and Faye Fisher**, former owners of the Dale Carnegie Training Franchise (Alberta, Canada)

"As one who has shared the grief and the blessings you describe in your book, I have no doubt you will touch and inspire so many others who travel this journey with us. You are a blessing, and your book is a gift to us all."

—**Trish Ellis**, International Communications Coordinator at Attitudinal Healing International

"Dr. Nieman consistently finds ways to create impressive and very helpful books. *Sustained* focuses on coping and advancing in positive ways from the most dramatically sad challenges you face, or will face, in your life. Thousands of people will benefit from reading this new very appealing book."

—**Daniel Kirschenbaum**, Ph.D., ABPP; Clinical Health & Sport Psychologist; Professor of Psychiatry & Behavioral Sciences, Northwestern University; former President, Division of Exercise and Sport Psychology, American Psychological Association

Also by Dr. Peter Nieman

Moving Forward: The Power of Consistent Choices in Everyday Life

101 Finish Lines

SUSTAINED

A Life Rewritten After Sudden Misfortune

DR. PETER NIEMAN

BALBOA.PRESS
A DIVISION OF HAY HOUSE

Balboa Press books may be ordered through booksellers or by contacting:

Balboa Press
A Division of Hay House
1663 Liberty Drive
Bloomington, IN 47403
www.balboapress.com
844-682-1282

Interior Image Credit: Dr. Peter Nieman

Print information available on the last page.

ISBN: 979-8-7652-4589-7 (sc)
ISBN: 979-8-7652-4590-3 (e)

Balboa Press rev. date: 10/16/2023

Contents

PART I

PART II

PART III

Foreword

"If we reject the painful, we only find more pain, but if we embrace what is within, if we peer fearlessly into the shadows – we stumble upon the light."
-Elizabeth Lesser

For the past twenty years, I have had the special privilege of working as a grief counsellor supporting parents who are facing the end of their child's life and parents who have had a child die. At the beginning of my career, I felt undeserving of counseling parents as they surrendered to the worst moment of their life. Despite having acquired a Master of Social Work with a specialization in grief and bereavement, I was not yet a parent and could not fully conceptualize the deep love and attachment that a parent has for their child, let alone the experience of the death of one. I have since been blessed with two boys and believe I am a better counsellor because of it. I have learned that you cannot do this work without combining your heart and human self with wisdom and knowledge. I remain humbled by the fact that I have not personally experienced this type of loss, however I have had the honour of holding space for over one thousand parents who have. My greatest learning has come from these brave humans that continue to be my teachers.

The grief parents experience is unique, desperate, devastating, and transformative. It is a pitch of grief unlike any other. My clients have described their grief as *sheer devastation, my worst nightmare, horrific, unbelievable, and the greatest tragedy imaginable.* In fact, most parents concur that there are no words to describe how out of order, unjust, unfair, and senseless the loss feels. A parent's world becomes shattered when a child dies. There is a brokenness at the core that is so overwhelming, words no longer hold accurate meaning.

Bereaved parents carry their children in the most profound ways, integrating them into every aspect of their being. This by far is the bravest act of parenting – caring for a child who is no longer physically present. It is the reflection of deep love and yearning that continues every day after they are gone. Parents do such a remarkable job of keeping their children's legacy alive that I truly feel like I know these beautiful children. This work has shown me how thin the veil is between this world and the one in which these children continue to exist. Bereaved parents forever straddle both worlds.

Grief does not change, bereaved parents do. This process has been described by some as a spiritual crisis. A life altering event that breaks parents open and leaves them to rebuild their framework of beliefs, worldviews, and sense of safety. I have witnessed the restructuring of self and the integration of grief, a process that initially seems impossible to the newly bereaved. I have seen these parents create meaning and a legacy out of the senseless loss. I have observed the chaos turn into order and direction, and parents learn to hold the duality of both joy and pain. I have watched countless parents step outside of their own grief and offer the newly bereaved compassion and the hope that they will survive. Moving from the darkness into the light is a remarkable shift, offering beauty and authenticity in the brokenness. I am grateful for the opportunity to bear witness to this process in Dr Nieman.

I remember feeling disbelief and heartache upon seeing Dr. Nieman's name on the referral. He is a well-known and respected pediatrician in our community. I remember thinking to myself, is there not an unwritten rule that protects those that spend their life caring for children, from losing one? If this could happen to Dr. Nieman, couldn't it happen to any one of us? The boundary that had protected me from parents in my program was somehow now invisible and the thread that connected us professionally, now became personal.

Following his loss, Dr. Nieman quickly gravitated towards the program, participating in both counseling and in grief group. I leaned in while he used his analytical and spiritual way of being in this world to understand and integrate his own grief and support his incredible wife, Dr. Zamonsky, and their surviving children. His faith was thoughtful and unwavering in the process, and every conversation manifested a teaching moment.

The Global Pandemic was a unique time for all of us. For many bereaved parents, it was a traumatic, uncertain, and isolating time filled with many secondary losses. In response to these challenges, my colleague Tara and I developed and executed virtual programming. For the first time in our program, we initiated grief groups on Zoom, including a 6-week grief group program, a monthly drop-in grief group and a novel loss by suicide group. Together, we transferred the connection and compassion found in face-to- face meetings and successfully created the same through a computer screen. While bearing his own pain, I watched as Dr. Nieman mentored and sustained other parents, often not even recognizing his gift.

Relationship and connection can help heal grief. Some of the most compassionate healers are wounded healers themselves. Dr. Nieman is one of those healers, a Wounded Warrior. A warrior who has not wasted his suffering. A warrior who has created magical connections in this madness of child loss. A warrior who uses his own wisdom and the teachings of Buddha, The Creator, Rabbis, and many others to elevate his understanding of compassion and purpose. A warrior who is humble and graceful. A warrior who shines his own light brightly so that others can see their path home. A warrior who helps us sustain hope and faith in the face of this tragedy.

If you are bereaved, if you are carrying a child in your heart, or if you are a companion to the bereaved, then you will find great meaning in this book. Dr. Nieman speaks bravely to the challenging and relevant issues surrounding mental health, suicide, and child loss. He eloquently moves us through the utter disbelief of finding his son Ben, his initial days of grief, the visitors that held him and the spiritual guides that taught him. He recounts these hours and days through his roles of family member, friend, mentor, spiritual student, and pediatrician, but there is no role more poignant in this story than his role as a bereaved father. He allows his readers to be intimate strangers to the most pivotal moments of his life, offering us the privilege of witnessing his raw grief.

This beautifully written work will capture you, guide you, validate you, and encourage you in the navigation of the tremendous complexities of loss. If you are supporting the bereaved, this book will enhance your grief literacy and build your capacity to sustain others around you. It underscores the devastating reality that child loss can happen to anyone, and most importantly, that you can survive it. It is a powerful story of hope and human connection.

Dr. Nieman, my heart is full because of Ben and all the other children that exist in this sacred space for me. I continue to be humbled and enlightened by you and the other parents that have graciously allowed me to share a few small steps on this path. I will forever be inspired by what you have taught me as a human, grief counsellor, and as a mother. You always believed in a purpose more powerful than the grief itself. You chose to let the grief reveal you. Thank you for your courage and vulnerability in inviting us on this spiritual journey through your book, ***Sustained***, where you have found your light in the shadows of grief.

Megan Miller, MSW RSW
Pediatric Hospice & Grief Support Program

Preface

The hardest day of my life, by far, unfolded one hour into 2020. One hour after I said goodbye to 2019, my life was abruptly and forever changed. My wife and I discovered the lifeless body of our youngest son, Benjamin, in our basement, where he chose to end his life. Ben died by suicide. He lost a long battle with depression. Ben decided to say goodbye to this world when he lost all hope. We never were given a chance to say goodbye to Ben.

We were plunged into a sudden, sickening tragedy. The door to an unexpected misfortune opened suddenly and we were instantly launched on a long winding path of an unchartered territory. A path marked by uncertainty and long dark nights; a path which took us around corners we never dreamt we would witness. Was this unexpected thrust into darkness *our* fate? Was it *my* lot? Who decided that it will be so? To this day I cannot say I am certain of the *exact* answer. But this I know experientially...I am sustained. My family is sustained, even though at times, we may not fully know it.

All humans, at some point in time, experience a definite fork in the road. Do we accept our fate? Do we agree with reality which spells it out plainly that, "It is so...it cannot be otherwise" Or... do we resist... and find that what we resist persists? Many among us, sadly, choose to fight reality by clinging tightly to the way we *insist* life should have been.

As an author, marathon runner and health coach, always focused on setting goals, reviewing years past and planning ahead. I anticipated the year 2020 to be a year of perfect vision. After all, the numbers matched what we want to hear when we see an eye doctor: "Your vision is perfect—20/20." On this day, my understanding of 20/20 vision was permanently changed.

Just Not My Vision

Little did I know my view of suffering in the days following a tragedy would be marked by 20/20 vision; just not the vision my plans called for. No human being ever fully has the capacity to grasp the root causes of deep suffering. The mystical aspects can be summarized by one single word: ineffable.

At best, one can only speculate; subscribe to a story that matches one's own biased beliefs. And hope that over time our interpretations pass the test of time. But so often our stories fail to pass the test of time, because they are either "My story" or "Our story," but *not* "THE Story."

In my own case, I came to the conclusion— after many sleepless nights, thinking about what happened to our family—that the timeless wisdom of Solomon, as expressed in Scriptures, indeed rings true.

In Proverbs 20:24 Solomon wrote that God directs our paths, and it is futile to try and figure everything out along the way. We can try. But we shall never *truly* know. Solomon reminded me that my path is directed by a Power far bigger and wiser than my finite brain capacity can comprehend.

Socrates once said that "The only wisdom is in knowing you know nothing." I cannot say that experiencing the loss of child taught me that I know nothing. I know way more than I did the day before Ben died. But I shall never know *everything* I need to know. I have sensed that there are indeed strong forces at work after major tragedies wound our brave hearts.

Joseph Goldstein, probably one of the most influential Buddhist teachers currently in North America, tells of a story in India when he was a young adult. He was directed to step away from buying an airline ticket at a counter in an airport. That decision led him to a part of India where he fell in love with the Buddha's teachings. Today, this compassionate wise teacher is revered. He continues to impact many of his students in their own quests to find freedom from suffering. Goldstein looks back at the trajectory of his life and comments that, "Sometimes there are strong forces at work in our lives."

It is a waste of time to try and figure everything out; instead, we trust wholeheartedly; we do not lean on our own limited understanding; we acknowledge the fact that we do not control as much as we think we do; we surrender and accept there is a Higher Power at work and then our paths will unfold as it should. (Paraphrased words describing Solomon's wisdom as expressed in Proverbs 3:5)

For most people who are plunged into a long dark tunnel of pain and despair, it is hard to resist the desire to have explanations of why bad things happen—often these tragedies happen to very good people who do not, according to our finite logic, see that as fair. Ultimately, we can only aspire to arrive at a place of radical acceptance. We can only stay open to what happens next, because we control far less than we think. This book is about this journey of knowing more, but I am accepting that I will never *fully* know; yet do I trust *fully*.

Surrender and accept radically. This is what psychologists call "conscious suffering." It takes a lot of inner work, but once we do that...our perceptions change. Henry David Thoreau wrote that it is not what you look at; it is what you see. Since Ben died, I have given the notion of free will much thought and in my own way of perceiving this imperfect world I look at...I see free will as one of the most important influencers of life's trajectories. Free will explains many of life's inevitable pain points.

Free Will

Our youngest son bravely battled depression and anxiety and at age sixteen, Ben used his free will and ended his life. My wife was the first one to discover his body two hours after midnight. Her agonizing cries coming out of our basement pierced us both as we embraced each other, next to Ben's lifeless body. That moment will forever reverberate in my memory. And yet, by Grace, I can confidently say I remain sustained and able to write about this from a place of authenticity.

Here is how this book is arranged:

> PART I talks about people sustaining us when we suffer. Ordinary human mediums are used to teach us what it means to receive the Love of an infinitely wise, loving, faithful Deity. In Part I you will meet other parents who also lost a dear child.

PART II talks about what I call the lonely times—often at 3 A.M. when one is wide awake and at the mercy of dark thoughts, feelings, and emotions. In Part II, I humbly share a few practical tools which consistently enable me to endure with joy. I pray some of my tools may also resonate for anyone who struggles to live a life after a tragic loss.

Part III of this book I want to talk about my own personal experiences of how the ever-present and limitless love of my Creator enables me to stay calm and strong in middle of a horrific storm.

In a spiritual book, *"A Course in Miracles"*, where lines between faith, metaphysics and psychology are blurred, a chapter lesson reads; "We are sustained by the Love of God." In part, that line led to the title of this book. (See Lesson 50 in *A Course in Miracles*)

A close and compassionate friend of mine was told about the title of the book. He asked me, "What does sustained mean?" At first, I thought he was joking. But he taught me that I must define the title.

According to various dictionary versions, to be sustained means: "to give support or relief to," or "to supply with sustenance," or "to be carried when under a weight or pressure," or "to support by adequate proof."

After our son transitioned from form to formless, we as a family, experienced all the above—we "tasted" the compassion of others and the Love of God. When we needed bread, we were given bread—not water. And when we were thirsty, we were given water--not bread.

My Name is Benjamin, but You Can Call Me Ben

In grade one Ben was diagnosed to be gifted, but only after his Kindergarten teacher suggested that he should repeat Kindergarten. Apparently, Ben was deemed as "odd" by this experienced teacher. When we heard her opinion, we were taken by surprise.

What exactly does odd mean? we thought.

My wife and I are physicians, and instead of wearing the hat of doctors, we decided to get Ben evaluated by an experienced and well-respected psychologist, who confirmed a diagnosis of his high intellect and ADHD (attention-deficit hyperactivity disorder).

In my career as a pediatrician, I encountered many Kindergarten students who tended to be very spontaneous and child-like in their behavior. Ben indeed was different—not odd, but different.

I shall never forget him as a four-year-old, in Mexico during Spring Break, floating in a pool on a cloudless day, going from person to person, in his usual friendly way, smiling mischievously, his light blond hair shining brightly in the blazing sunshine, and announcing with enthusiasm to *total* strangers, "Hello...my name is Benjamin, but you can call me Ben."

Writing this brings tears to my eyes and pains my heart. Yet my heart is not broken; it is still in one piece. The loss of Ben traumatized my heart. But by the Grace of God, I was given an unbreakable heart early in my life when I became curious about the inner workings some mistakenly refer to as "religion." Even though I faithfully showed up for spiritual work, I wish I could share with you that my heart is healed. It is not so. It carries a scar... forever... because that is what losing a child does to anyone's heart.

"My name is Benjamin, but you can call me Ben." Those were the words at the end of his obituary, and etched on the side of the urn where his ashes are kept on the desk of his bedroom—a room *to this day* where things are left, just as they were the day he finally lost his battle with depression.

We keep the door closed. My wife, Corinne, never enters that room. Occasionally, I may open the door, spend only a few minutes in Ben's room, and notice all the evidence of a teenage boy: I see his books, his homework, his backpack, an empty soda bottle, his drawings, his Lego creations, and his favorite shoes—Vans. On his bed lies a rugby jersey with the letters BN etched on the back. You will read more later of how that jersey got there in his room.

My only comfort is to know that he is free from suffering, and according to my faith, in the Presence of a Higher Power and a loving God. Eternal life started for Ben shortly after midnight on that fateful day. And one day, I will catch up to Ben again and spend a forever-future with him and my loved ones in a perfect, peace-soaked Heaven. The memories of this imperfect world shall fade and become dimmer and dimmer, moment by moment.

Meanwhile

Before I get to catch up with Ben one day, I would need to have to answer the invitation as to how I want to live my life without him. All of us, without exception, will at some point of our lives, receive the invitation of navigating huge losses. Change is a given. Life can be hard at times and as we read in an important book by Scott Peck, life is hard for all (See *The Road Less Travelled (2) in Bibliography).*

Along the way, we all need wisdom, and for some of us it happens the way an ancient philosopher Aeschylus wrote when he penned these words:

> *He who learns must suffer. And even in our sleep pain that cannot forget falls drop by drop upon the heart, and in despair, against our will, comes wisdom by the awful grace of God.*

To suffer means to undergo. As the pain of the loss of a child falls drop by drop upon heavy hearts, we undergo change. It is a messy change, but also a change which purifies and matures us into gaining more wisdom—even when it unfolds against our will.

I was told by an articulate author that initially grief is like a raging fire, but later it becomes like a warm hearth. I cannot say that the latter is true for me. My trauma is still relatively fresh.

My hope in writing this book is that you may be prompted to consider your own preparation of what to do when *your* invitation to suffer arrives; or perhaps before that happens, you may be called upon to help another fellow being feel how it feels to be sustained during a dark night of the soul.

Compare a life to a beautiful cup or plate. One wishes it will never break and fall apart. But sometimes it does. And some say it certainly will. It is just a matter of time before the sacred beauty gets shattered into pieces. What to do then? Throw it away or do what is known as *Kintsugi*?

Kintsugi

Not long after Ben left our home for his new Home in Heaven, I learned about a Japanese word, Kintsugi. It is a Japanese art form which dates to the 15th century. When cups and plates broke, masters repaired them in an unusual way.

Instead of using glue, the cups or plates are made better. The broken places are not glued together. Instead, in the broken parts, the masters use a special lacquer mixed with gold and silver. This way the scars of the break are made into something beautiful. It describes the scars of my heart.

As parents, we have experienced some form of brokenness. We have been glued together, and yet separately, because parental grief unfolds differently after a child dies. At the time of this writing, we are not at the same stage of grieving. We never descended into the dark nights of the soul totally alone; we are almost never transformed alone. As the famous Trappist monk, Thomas Merton, observed, "All humans are interconnected in some way or form. They simply may not know it yet."

Though caring people who met us in our time of need and by a Source whose strength is unlimited...Corinne and I have found ways to move forward, one step at a time. Limping along but restored. Knocked down but not knocked out. Scars can be made beautiful –just like the Kintsugi art of the Japanese.

Experiential Knowing

Beginnings determine trajectories.

With that in mind, I must make sure that you know my bias based on personal experiences related to deep sufferings: all things *do not always work out* for the good and that a good outcome which supposedly is certain to those who love their Creator is *not* always true. The notion that patience will settle all suffering *right now,* this very moment, is a myth and a set up for more suffering after a child has died.

The immediacy of an unexpected loss makes all parents unreceptive to such words—even when the words ultimately, much later may ring true. My advice to anyone who sincerely attempt to encourage a parent who buried a child is to avoid platitudes and cliches.

People who teach these idealistic beliefs may not have lost a child. Unless one has a child or loses a child... one never knows why most parents fear the loss of a child more than anything else. It is difficult to see how losing a child can end up as a good thing.

Suffering cannot be stopped dead in its tracks by patience or prayer. As James Finley discovered after the death of his dear wife, Maureen, "I cannot pray away the pain of my wife's death. I cannot pray my sadness away. But I can learn to pray in the midst of my sadness and listen to it and see what it has to teach me about life, and love and whatever. So, prayer is not a remedy for getting rid of difficult situations."

I promise that platitudes "sold" by Pied Pipers, with zero experience, mean nothing to parents who have lost a child. In fact, they have no patience for well-meaning souls whose intentions are good: intentions manifesting as "advice" often given before all the facts are clear. Well-meaning "advice" may be rooted in pure motives, and still not be helpful at all.

I have experienced the loss of a child. Every page I wrote in this book is based on my personal *experience*. A famous author of New York Times best-selling books once said, "Unless you write from your heart you are merely typing the words."

I have written about these experiences, my family's experiences, and about what I learned from other parents who have also lost a child. Just like me.

I trust that once you close this book when you come to the end, you will ponder further in your heart, regarding the issue of dealing with sudden change and loss, and you may want to prepare for inevitable changes that will unfold at some point. I tried to write from the heart.

Dedicated to Ben and our Second Family

Some refer to parents who have lost a child as "A club nobody wants to belong to." These are the parents whose child was alive one day …and then forever gone. An abrupt finality took place which forever alters hopeful trajectories. The child who once had a future, is now lifeless, and futureless, and parents are left to deal with this sickening aftermath.

This book is dedicated to my brave and highly intelligent son, Ben, and to the parents of our amazing grief support group I refer to as: "My second family" (also known at times as "The Wednesday Warriors") Through these words my hope is that you will get to know more about Ben and my second family.

This group has taught me and my wife about communal grief in more ways that any author, grief expert or skilled therapist cannot even come close—unless they travelled on the same path after experiencing the same sickening tragedy. Living forever without a sweet, innocent, dear child who left the planet with so much potential still to be realized, is one of the toughest—if not *the* toughest—assignments. These are my friends who, forever at anniversaries, graduations, weddings will experience moments of, "I wonder what would..."

> *I wonder what my child would have done by now had they stayed alive. I wonder what they may have accomplished. I wonder who they would have married. I wonder what they would have said about this or that.*

This group has brought tears of joy to my hurting heart. They have taught me much about the capacity of human beings to adjust to adversity. Each one of these loving parents experienced what it means to slowly recover after the burial of a dear child.

I salute you as my teachers— your consistent and wise teachings on how we walk each other home is stored deeply in my chest. You have taught me by your kindness how it is possible for good to outshine the bad. You have become my heroes. Your example of love and wisdom nourishes, like a vital artery, my wide-open receptive heart. With my hand over my heart, and my back bent forward...I bow to you. Destiny arranged for you to be sent into my fragile and broken life, now showing the golden scars of Kintsugi.

I will forever be changed. I intend to always walk in gratitude. It is a huge honour for me to share your stories with the rest of our world.

I see the light in you which is also in me; we *all* are potential salt and light deliverers, for when we warrior together as a group, we do it not only for ourselves and each other; we do it to show the world what true resilience really looks like.

CALGARY
CANADA
2023

PART I

1

What No Parent Wants to Experience

Nothing will ever test one's faith more than experiencing a senseless loss.
—Rick Warren

I tend to be a creature of habit and my ritual for December 31 is always the same. I see patients until noon in my clinic, and then head back home to spend quality time with my dear family. Even though I tend to do most of my daily running early in the day, I often go out for second workout after I finish working at my clinic.

The sun was shining brightly on December 31, 2019. A New Year was a few hours away and this year I thought was going to be different. The number, 2020, caught my attention. As I enjoyed my second run that day, being in a flow state, I reflected on the profound lack of happiness of my son Ben, who had a difficult 2019. I felt confident that, based on the way he bravely battled his assignment of being burdened by deep depressive states, 2020 would be a better year.

I saw 2020 as a symbolic number— perfect vision. Accurate perceptions.

Perception sets the stage. It is indeed critical to become aware of how we view our lives. It has been said that with our thoughts we create our outcomes. At least that is what Dr. Wayne Dyer so often taught with his deep conviction, that it if we get what we do not want, it is usually because of our own inability to attract and manifest the best.

Dyer was fond of reminding his followers that "When we change the way we look at things, the things we look at change." I am not sure if Dr. Wayne Dyer originated that expression or paraphrased it—perhaps he borrowed it from an ancient sage or Eastern wisdom. It may not matter who produced this wisdom. Our thoughts and perceptions do matter—especially how we think after tragedy strikes.

During my run I was reminded of the deeper meaning of the words, "When you change the way you look at things, the things you look at change." I expected 2020 to be a year of purer perceptions.

Upon arriving home, still drenched in sweat, but energized by my workout and the certainty that 2020 would be a pivotal year, I stopped at the door of Ben's room. I noticed he was working on his laptop. Curiously, I asked him, "Ben what are you working on?"

"I am just making a few notes Dad," he answered, beaming out his usual wry smile. He always tended to have a sense of humor that both entertained, but also made one wonder in confusion at times. My wife and Ben often laughed at how easy it was for him to use his humor in ways where I did not know what to do next.

I wanted to give him his space and did not inquire further. Teenagers can be easily irritated at times, when parents impose upon them when they are not yet ready. I followed up with, "Ben, I am so proud of you and the way you have handled all your troubles the past year. I am really looking forward to spending time with you in 2020. I am also so glad that you will be celebrating with your friends tonight." He was invited to join his friends for New Years Eve.

He looked at me and paused. I thought he looked calm and relaxed when he uttered these words, "Thanks Dad. I am also looking forward to spending time with you."

Ben did not have many friends. It always bothered my wife more than it bothered me. In hindsight I now know that for a teenager, friends matter a great deal. This knowledge came to me too late. Too late to change anything in my own family, but never too late for my patients when I hear from them, "I have no friends."

With this as background, I was glad that Ben and some of his "close" friends made plans to spend the evening together. He had dinner with us, and then his friend and the friend's father were supposed to pick him up at 10 PM.

My wife and I got invited to see in the new year of 2020 at our neighbour's home. We said goodbye to Ben around 9 PM on December 31, 2019, and hugged him, glad that finally he was going to enjoy quality time with friends. Little did we know at the moment, that would be the last time we would ever get to hug our son. At that moment he was present; in a few hours he would be gone.

Around midnight we texted Ben. He explained that his friends stood him up and he was still at home. He told us he was fine and resisted a suggestion for him to join us next door. To this day, my wife blames herself for not physically getting Ben and bringing him to the neighbour's home. I doubt she will ever be able to forgive herself or forgive us as parents.

Before Ben's passing, I knew extraordinarily little about suicide. All I knew is what I learned at the American Academy of Pediatrics. I never lost a patient to suicide after 36 years of being a pediatrician.

I was told a risk factor for ending a life is a previous attempt. Ben engaged in cutting. He also tried to hang himself a few years prior to the fateful evening of December 31. Despite excellent psychiatric care, all changed just after midnight and a few hours into the 2020.

In retrospect I had 2020 vision. He made plans to end his life days before he actually executed his plan successfully. It brought him a sense of relief that his suffering was about to end. His calm demeanor fooled me. What I perceived to be progress, was in fact a red flag which I never recognized.

We did all we could do to support him during his chronic depression years. We took him to see a very skilled psychiatrist; he was on a number of medications; we took him to counsellors and therapists; we tried our best to encourage him and love him. We told him that we had the faith he would get through his dark seasons.

Although Ben once made a commitment to follow the teachings of Christ and although a dear pastor friend of ours became a mentor to Ben, he seemed to be questioning his faith toward the end of his life. I suspect as a teen seeking his identity, he probably wondered how a loving God can be so cruel as to allow suffering and fail to alleviate it.

Ben also enjoyed staying up late and when we returned home just after 1 AM, we called out his name. He was not in his room. He was not by the TV where he so often watched movies.

He was where my wife found him in the basement.

When I heard her agonizing shrieks, I rushed down and came upon a scene which no parent ever wants to see. My wife held on to one of Ben's lifeless legs. She looked up at me with huge anxious eyes and said, "I cannot live any longer—this is too much."

I told her, "We shall get through this together." I held her tight, and we left the area to go upstairs. I then called the police.

When I told her "We shall get through this together," I meant the two of us.

The Siblings

When our son Jon came home a few hours after Ben passed, I had to tell him in the best way possible. There is no easy way to do something like that. My wife was in the home with some of the EMS staff and compassionate police officers. Outside the house were a few police cars. The police officer with me suggested that I tell Jon the catastrophic news that he lost his brother before he entered the house.

I met Jon as he was coming up our driveway and upon hearing the news, he immediately fell to his knees. A short while later he got up fast and started to walk off into the dark night. I tried to stop him, but the police officer told me to just leave Jon alone, because he needed his own space. I worried about his safety for as long as he was gone and gave him a long hug upon his return.

Ben's sister Katie and brother Matthew, both live in British Columbia. I decided not to call them, but to ensure, first of all via people who knew them, that they would not be alone when they got the news. I am glad that while making these tough decisions, and while still being in a state of shock and disbelief, my mind was guided by a Force marked by infinite wisdom and infinite love. I was sustained while dazed by the new reality.

At the time I did not realize how much I was supported by this unseen Power. It is one thing to be told that we are never alone. But there are times where it may seem that a loving God is either far away or does not exist at all.

It is extremely comforting to personally experience the benevolence of the Creator of my children, who cared about me and them, and directed all of us more than we shall ever fully know.

Everyone flew back home, and together, we prepared Ben's memorial service. Our son-in-law Caleb, helped Katie, our only daughter, look for photos of Ben. We would use in the days ahead to place in his obituary, and on the screen in the church where a community would gather to remember this young man loaned to our family for only 16 years.

Jon prepared a speech all by himself. He bravely delivered his ideas about this situation five days later. It contained one or two profanities which caught some by surprise, but made others laugh. The latter group later told me that Jon's authenticity impressed them. He sure did not wear a mask and spoke from his heart, about the loss of his younger brother. Profanities uttered by Jon, standing next to the podium in a big church, packed with mourners were somehow forgiven that day.

Little did I know that although it takes a village to raise a child, it also takes a village to bury a child. We were about to discover the true meaning of how a global village reached out to us in the aftermath. We were indeed launched on a new path of discovering that the Love of God sustains us. Together meant a community of kind people. Together meant people who taught me all I know about being sustained. Getting through it all, together, was not just me and my wife, but a community of compassionate souls.

A few days after Ben died, and about four days before the memorial service in a church, a female funeral director was at our door to guide us through the process of writing an obituary. Janine entered our lives with a sorrowful but brave heart. She is the part-owner of one of our city's largest funeral homes and rarely conducted funerals herself, but for us she was prepared to make an exception.

This was the first time in my life where I had to write an obituary. Janine guided us skillfully and helped us write Ben's obituary which read:

OBITUARY OF BENJAMIN JOSHUA NIEMAN

May 23, 2003 - Calgary, Alberta
January 1, 2020 - Calgary, Alberta

"My name is Benjamin, but you can call me Ben."

It is with heavy hearts that we say good-bye to Ben Nieman who passed away on Wednesday, January 1, 2020, at the age of 16 years.

> Ben followed in his sister and two brothers' footsteps when he was born and delivered at the Rockyview General Hospital by Dr. Walter Moscovitz, for whom we are so thankful for his care to our children. His first ten years of education were spent at Glenmore Christian Academy. There were many teachers who had influence on Ben's life, we would like to give special acknowledgement to Mrs. Nath, Mr. Ness, Mr. Reist, Mr. Robertson, Mrs. Allan, and Mr. Hielema who had a profound impact on Ben's life. Ben was able to be the basketball team manager, which meant a lot to him as this was a way for him to fit in with the other kids.
>
> In grade ten he moved to Henry Wise Wood High School, where he excelled in math and played on the junior rugby team. Ben was a beautiful person on the outside; he taught us how to love unconditionally no matter how unique you are. He had a very sensitive spirit, and because of this he would carry the burdens of many people and at times because of his struggle with mental health he had difficulty processing them. He battled with ADD and depression and we are proud of him because this was a daily battle, but he fought hard. Ben is now at peace and now those of us that are left behind will fight to navigate our life without Ben. His high intelligence and dry sense of humor were traits that we will remember him for.

*****

One of my friends, Israel Lachovsky, who calls himself "The Jewish Santa" because he looks like Santa and loves to play that role every Christmas in various community settings commented, "We can only attempt to honour Ben's memory by regarding with awe, the beautiful words that you shared with the community as expressed in his obituary."

2

Mr. Roger's Twin

When I was a boy and would see scary things in the news, my mother would say to me, "Look for the helpers. You will always find people who are helping."
—Fred Rogers

Ray Matheson could have been the twin brother of Mr. Fred Rogers, the TV personality who for years hosted the show *"Mr. Rogers' Neighborhood."*

I discovered Mr. Roger's show for children by accident. Although some parents found Fred Rogers "boring," I was attracted by his calm, compassionate, wise, and loving demeanor.

Every time I heard Fred say, "We love you just the way you are," I knew he truly meant it. He taught about kindness, what to do with the anger inside and often shared a story of how his mother told him that when there is huge trouble, to always look for the helpers.

During the tragic unfolding of 911 and the collapse of the Twin Towers in New York City, we saw first-hand what that meant—looking for the helpers.

The way Mr. Rogers talked is the way Ray talks. He has a calm and sincere voice; a voice which brings immediate comfort. Ray's love toward all human beings remains unconditional and embodies the words of Christ who said that as much as we did virtuous deeds to the least among us, we did it unto Him. Ray radiates Christ-like qualities wherever he goes.

This compassionate minister fully understands what it means to allow the generosity of God to flow through him to others.

A few hours after Ben died, I did not want to call Ray and wake him up with the news of our tragic loss. I waited for the police to deal with what happened. This took close to five hours to be accomplished. They were indeed many helpers in police uniform. A few weeks after this fateful night I wrote a letter of thanks to the police chief of our city. He wrote back. Tears filled my eyes as I read his note *thanking us* for allowing these fine men and women in uniform to serve us that night.

Sunrise

Soon after sunrise, I called Ray and shared what happened to us. Anyone who feels there are no good pastors, never met Ray. To me and my wife, Ray represents the best example of how to be Christ-like in our dealings with others. Ray is one of the few people I know who consistently exhibits virtues such as love, joy, peace, patience, goodness, kindness, faithfulness, gentleness, and self-control.

Very shortly after taking my call, Ray was at our front door.

Understandably, as I look back today, I was in shock. Much of what happened hours after our loss became a blur. It felt surreal. I held up strong all through the darkness, but when the sun rose, I felt numb. I could tell I had very little fuel left in my resilience tank.

What I clearly remember though was how Ray's calm and loving presence reassured us. We felt the energy of his compassion and love.

People who met the Dalai Lama tell us that being in his presence made them feel that they were the only ones that mattered at that moment. They felt the undivided attention of a spiritual teacher. While Ray ministered to our sorrows and needs with utmost kindness, we felt the same way. He was fully present and calm. To this very day Ray checks in on us and often asks us, "How are you doing and how are your hearts?"

Seemingly Forgotten

In my first book, *Moving Forward,* I wrote about a familiar poem called *Footprints*. It is about a story of two sets of footprints along the way, one next to the other. At some point there is only one set of footprints. The author of the poem makes a point that during tough times there were two footprints—those of the writer going through suffering and those of God walking beside him. But why did two sets become only one? Did God abandon the writer? How could a loving God be there and suddenly leave us alone to suffer by ourselves?

The disappointment of being abandoned turned into joy when the author was told that there was only one set of footprints, because at the time of only one set of footprints he was carried by a loving Father, a Higher Power, a God some call "Abba Father" --which means the same as the word "Daddy." Sometimes when we take the time to see and fully attend, we not only see but experience the love of God via people like Ray who are sent to us in times of need.

The Healers Prayer

In *A Course in Miracles,* we learn about the Healers Prayer.

This powerful and life-changing prayer starts by saying, "We are here only to be truly helpful. We are here to represent Him who sent us."

As the sun shone brightly on the first day in 2020, I sensed Ray was there to be truly helpful. He was there to represent the One who sent him. My family was not alone. Helpers were sent to our home. We were sustained by the love of God.

When Ray prayed with me and my wife, he reminded us to recall the powerful words of the Psalmist who wrote, "God is our refuge and strength, a very present help in times of trouble" (Psalm 46).

Ray indeed understood what it means when one allows God to teach us to be of help in this troubled and imperfect world.

3

The Rabbi

The best way to eulogize the deceased is to
let their good deeds speak for them.
—Rebbe Menachem Mendel Schneerson

Rabbi Matusof and his wife were the next members of the village who showed up at our door to help us. Their knock on the front door left me speechless. News of my son's passing must have spread fast into our community. I invited them into our family room, and we sat down and listened to a story the Rabbi shared.

The Rabbi's first words were, "I am sorry for your loss. We will pray for wisdom and strength." His eyes matched his words. I knew it came from deep within his compassionate and wise heart. Many years of preparing to serve as a Rabbi, and many years of ministering to the various needs of those who suffer, Rabbi Matusof radiated wisdom. He is known as a man who is not judgmental, and yet one who knows how to discern with compassion, kindness, and wisdom.

In Judaism the word for charity and justice is *tzedakah*. I heard about it prior to Ben's passing; I experienced one sunny afternoon, sometime between his death and burial, when Menachem Matusof knocked on our door.

The Rabbi did exactly what his own role model and teacher, Rebbe Menachem Mendel Schneerson, taught him to do which is to not try and explain anything, but to be with the ones who mourn; to soothe them and console them. Rebbe Schneerson taught that there is nothing one can really say, for no matter, how we might try, we must accept that we often do not understand G-d's mysterious ways.

To this day I still can close my eyes and relive our time with the Rabbi and his wife. We were seated in our living room one wintry afternoon, early in January 2020. The sunshine streamed dimly across the quiet room. There were long moments of silence and a deep knowing. A mystical moment which is hard to explain, and yet a moment described in Scripture by these words: "Be still… and *know* that I am G-d" (Out of respect for the Jewish tradition I am not typing God, but G-d).

He went on to tell various stories which perfectly resonated with me. One story was about another Rabbi who also lost a child.

I Give Him Back to You

This Rabbi accompanied the coffin containing his dead child to a plane, which was to carry his child to a synagogue in Eastern Canada. The Rabbi, a mourning father, when handing over the coffin to strangers, said this to his Heavenly Father: "G-d… you gave me this child, and now I give him back to you."

This story, as told by the Rabbi, has stayed with me over the years since my son made his transition. I can imagine that there may be parents who believe that there is no G-d. To hear that their child does not belong to them, and that they are to be at peace with the idea that the child was on loan to them, may not go over well at all. In fact, it may make them terribly angry, and even bitter, cynical, and jaded.

To explain to such a parent, "G-d you gave me this child and now I give him back to you" is a bit like explaining to someone the taste of salt when they have never tasted salt.

I remain thankful that I met the Matusof family—originally as patients—and I am deeply grateful that the Rabbi and I share a common trust in Hashem --another Hebrew name for G-d.

They Don't Belong to Us; They Come Through Us

The wound and the surreal feelings associated with the finality of a dead child were all so fresh that afternoon.

We *easily* forget that our children are not ours; they are lent to us for whatever reason we are allotted with them. A Source who defies understanding gracefully lend them to us. We are mere stewards.

One of the most spiritually influential writers of all time, Kahlil Gibran, in his timeless book, *The Prophet,* said that children **don't belong** to us, but come **through** us. (Words I made bold to underscore its truth).

When I read Gibran's words for the first time in 1982, before I became a parent, it was if I was told how salt tastes. Now that I heard the Rabbi's story of how we give our children back to the Source, I *understand* what salt tastes like.

Ben came through me and his mom; he did not belong to us. We were only asked to care for him and love him the best way we knew to do that.

I reflected on why we identify with our children so very deeply. They define us—or so we think; we allow it even when we must learn to not let that happen. We would sacrifice endlessly because we love them so deeply. When they suffer, we suffer. As so many other grieving mothers have taught me, the human tendency is to blame ourselves first when something bad happens to or children—even when it was not our fault at all.

Interconnected

Over the years I have been privileged to get invited to many of the Matusof's Bar Mitzvahs and weddings. Without exception, *each* event underlined to me the meaning of Ubuntu.

There are times when in extra measure we become aware of how our lives are interconnected. We experience what Africans call "Ubuntu" which means we discover and know how much we need each other. This is humanness. And as author and Buddhist teacher, Jack Kornfield once said, "It is ok to be human."

The Rabbi and I are always in the Presence of a Creator who loves *all* his children. As children we all belong.

It is so quite easy to forget the Source of all that is good and perfect. Just as we are not always aware of the air we breathe in; we are not always aware of the source of the air— a Higher Power. Or as some Buddhists call it, "A Strong force at work."

This Power or unseen Force is to me not *just* a Higher Power, but *THE Highest Power*—far above all other spiritual powers. A Power far above tradition, organized religion, philosophies, or any book written by a New York Times bestselling spiritual guru.

The Rabbi always jokes with me by saying he came to me in my office expecting to get a Rx (prescription), and instead I gave him a Rx (reminder) of a verse from Psalms or Proverbs.

Before Ben died, I remember when the Rabbi brought his kids to see me in my clinic having many deep spiritual conversations with him—back and forth. I remember sharing that we have a source of hope who generously gives us peace and joy as we trust in Him, and the same Source then fills us with hope, to overflowing, by the power of G-d.

Always at Work and Unseen

This Divine Spirit guides and comforts us always. It is at work when we sleep; our nails grow *even* as we sleep; the rest of our bodily functions continue under the direction of what doctors call the autonomic nervous system. But who controls such miracles?

It becomes clear once we raise our own and collective consciousness to a higher level, that such intricate designs cannot be an accident known as "Nature without a source."

The Rabbi was well aware of G-d's role in all of our living.

A few days after the Rabbi's visit, I was running one morning and seemingly out of nowhere, I was reminded of the comforting words in the Old Testament; where G-d says, "My mercies are new every morning. Great is my faithfulness."

Rabbi Matusof has not forgotten to check in at times, no sooner did I get home and my phone rang. It was the Rabbi. Without me telling him about my experience during my run, he reminded me of...you can guess...G-d's mercies are new every morning. His faithfulness is great.

That day, the same comforting message was sent to me from two sources —just in case I may have missed it or taken it for granted. This was enough evidence for me that a mysterious and unseen Power is always at work on our behalf.

Shalom

Later, during a time of deep contemplative prayer, I was reminded of a verse in the Old Testament, a book the Rabbi knows so well.

The Prophet Isaiah reminds the reader that we are kept in constant and perfect Shalom when we keep our hearts and minds on Hashem; when we commit ourselves to Him; lean on Him; and hope confidently in Him. (Isaiah 26:3)

Only those who walked though fires, who felt the heat and yet whose hair never got burned; whose clothes do not smell like smoke...only those are the ones among us who understand Divine Peace which when experienced makes fighting over theological man-made dogmas far less relevant.

Just before the Rabbi and his dear wife left, he handed me a book as a gift. It was a book written by an influential and wise man in the Rabbi's faith tradition, Rebbe Menachem Mendel Schneerson. The title of the book is *Toward a Meaningful Life.*

Inscribed in the front of the book I read: "Dear Dr. Nieman, with friendship and deep care. May G-d be the source of comfort and strength. One act of goodness and kindness will change the world." One act of goodness by the Rabbi that day will forever be etched in my memory. To this day the Rabbi and his wife inspire me by the way they care for all people.

The Rabbi's visit reminded me that if we have faith and if we follow rules, it is good. But to love one another is even better. Our faith is embodied by our deeds of lovingkindness. That wintery afternoon, a few days after our son's transition, when the Matusofs knocked on our door, was a reminder of G-d's kindness.

***

The day we had a memorial to honour Ben remains mostly a blur. Perhaps because I have cultivated the habit of journaling daily since 1992, I am able to write the next chapter.

4

The Memorial

We are under pressure on every side, but never without a way out; we are at our wits end, but never at our hope's end; we are never abandoned by God. We are knocked down, but never knocked out.
—2 Corinthians 4:8-9

When it was time to have a memorial service for Ben at the church we regularly attended, something interesting happened as we waited for the vehicle provided by the funeral service to escort us to the service. My phone lit up.

I saw a text from a man called Kyle. It read: "I may be a few minutes late but if you see a guy in a suit at the back of the church it is me". My jaw dropped. This text was from Kyle Yesuda who lives in Seattle. At the time Kyle was also the President of the American Academy of Pediatrics.

Regardless of his busy schedule in his role as the President of the American Academy of Pediatrics, he decided to fly to Canada and be there for Ben's funeral.

Suddenly I remembered that when we discovered Ben's lifeless body and I told my wife "We will get through this", I did not fully grasp at *that* moment the deep truth coming out of my mouth, almost prophetically.

We were never going to be alone. We would get through this tragic and senseless loss with the compassionate support of a wide variety of other human beings.

People Care

People like Kyle would express to us and the world that inside all humans is a certain amount of goodness. A type of "God-ness"

At Ben's memorial we experienced love embodied in the flesh, rather than on a paper or hypothetically taught from a pulpit.

When we stood in the receiving line following the church service to remember Ben, Kyle came up to us and hugged us with a heart big enough to contain many others. His eyes teared up. We hugged again. I knew I was forever going to be sustained by the Love of God. To this day Kyle and I carry each other's burdens when we meet, usually via phone. Since that day at our church, Kyle has experienced his own share of suffering. He received a diagnosis of a neurological condition for which there is no cure.

An email arrived before Ben's memorial service. It was from the principal of his old school. The email reassured us that the school will continue to stand in prayer with our family. The principal added, "I just read Ben's obituary—such a positive statement of Ben's intellect, humor, and heart. We will be standing behind you in support on Monday at the church."

The unimaginable loss of a child causes one to limp for the rest of one's life. We move forward. Time does not heal the limp. It is a chronic limp; one has no choice in accepting it as one's lot in life. The limp is associated with an inner pain which is hard to grasp unless one also lost a child. An author whose writings always stir the heart, Mirabai Starr, observed that "Grief is for a lifetime, and it is as if we learn to surf again without the limb we once had."

As my wife and I prepared what we wanted a pastor to read on our behalf, we wrote out our thoughts. There was no way we could stand in front of over seven hundred people and read it ourselves. We asked Pastor Ray Matheson to read it. And he did just that—with sensitivity and love.

This is what we wrote and what Ray read on our behalf:

> *We are so grateful and humbled that you chose to be here with us today.*
>
> *Many of you have told us that what happened came as a shock, and you are so sorry for our immense pain; words cannot describe the emotions we are dealing with; we know that many*

are praying and that you offered to help us with anything—all we need to do is call.

We are told that God is love. His love is poured all over us through your amazing kindness toward us.

Since we discovered this huge loss, we learned this:

The Bible teaches us that He is present at the time of trouble and that He is close to the broken hearted.

That is true. We experienced it—even now and in the days ahead we lean on Him and not our own understanding. We are perplexed but not in despair. We are knocked down but not destroyed. We are pressed on all sides but not crushed. (2 Cor 4:8-9)

We want to thank the pastors at First Alliance and the pastor who married us in 1990—Pastor Len Zoeteman—-for the way they represented our Heavenly Father. We are comforted by their words, their visits—more than once. They represented Christ Jesus in an amazing manner.

Without our friends in faith, we would have collapsed under the weight of our pain.

In addition, all our friends at work, people who helped Ben, people who know us well and those who took the time, from various parts of the world, to reach out just to show care... ... we honour you and love you.

Jesus is our Savior; saving us not just from our mistakes but from falling apart and He is our mentor on how to genuinely love one another.

Benjamin Joshua Nieman was not always called by that name. Already having a girl and then two boys, we were hoping for a girl to balance out our family. For almost nine months we called him Emily. Well, that was not what God had planned for us. A little boy arrived. When we called home to tell the kids, Katie cried and said "why did it have to be another boy. I wanted a girl and I wanted to call her Paprika." —one of the characters in the Blue's Clues kids show. When they arrived at the hospital later, it was love at first sight and she became the best big sister any brother could ask for.

Ben was an outgoing friendly child. One spring break when he was about four, he would float around the pool at our Mexican resort in his little car floaty going up to perfect strangers saying "Hi, my name is Benjamin, but you can call me Ben."

He started his schooling at the Love of Learning Preschool with his teacher Mrs. Nath. He gave her a run for her money. Once when she decided to take a much-needed vacation from teaching to go on a trip to the Caribbean she gave the substitute teacher strict instructions not to call her unless it was an emergency. She had barely reached her destination when a call came from the school. Ben had been misbehaving badly and the substitute did not know what to do. Ben insisted that they call Mrs. Nath. After getting her on the phone she discovered that the reason Ben had to call was to make sure that she was not going to get kidnapped by the Pirates of the Caribbean. After some discussion and thought they both agreed that she was much too scary for any pirates to even think of kidnapping her.

Ben moved from there on to Glenmore Christian Academy. He was smart beyond his years and had struggles at times to fit in and make friends. His sense of humor often was above his peers but some of his teachers really clicked with him and made him feel special. Mr. Ness really appreciated their private jokes. Mr. Reist set up a Lego club which consisted of Ben, Mr. Reist and no one else. When other kids got wind of this and wanted to join, Ben said no. He wanted it to be his Lego time only. We know he was loved and cared for there and we were supported through some very tough times. He was able to be the official manager of the basketball team, a position that Ben created himself. He was known to give some awesome motivational speeches possibly with some words that were not suitable for a Christian school.

Ben looked forward to moving on to high school. He hoped to find some friends that lived closer to him so he could ride his bike and hang out with other kids. He excelled in math and was able to help others with their math homework. He maintained excellent marks even though we rarely saw him study at home. He joined the junior rugby team. When we told one of the coaches that it was the first time, he had ever played on a team sport he said "Yes, we can tell." We laughed, but they made him feel welcome and part of the team. We think it was because he was so skinny and tall, he was easy to lift up in the lineout. The coach was looking forward to having him on the team again this year and taking him on the rugby trip to Ireland.

In the past year or so, Ben wanted to get a snake. We said absolutely not. He came up with suggestions for all kinds of pets including mice, guinea pigs, and hedgehogs. Having a cat, we did not think those were good ideas. In the end we settled on a cactus that he named Phil. We thought it was a good compromise. Ben... not so much.

Ben was a very picky eater all his life. On our spring break trips to Mexico he ate nothing but cheeseburgers and fries for two weeks. He loved fast food and candy. Luckily for him we lived within blocks of McDonald's, Subway, A & W, Little Caesar's, a donair shop, and a convenience store. Often Ben would ask for a ride to get a late-night snack or stock up on some food for the weekend. He would then proceed to play video games and eat pizza and candy and never gain an ounce.

We now know his inner pain is over and he is with our loved ones who already passed over to the other realm—the bliss of life after death in the presence of LOVE.

Mr. Fred Rogers who hosted Mister Rogers' Neighborhood once said that when we face a crisis... ....ALWAYS look for the helpers. We know it is true because of what we have encountered since Ben left. In fact, the helpers came to us in so many ways.

We pray that nobody in this room will ever forget to look for the helpers in their own time of need.

And we pray that these words Jesus spoke will mean something to each and every one present:

> *Peace I give you... ....my peace I give you....not as the world gives do I give to you....let not your hearts be troubled; neither let it be afraid.*

Thank you all for being here today as a way to say "WE CARE"

Ben lost his battle against depression and lost hope in the end. We are so proud of Ben who was left under our care as his parents for 16 years and 7 months. He was an amazing son, smart, caring, and with a crazy, sarcastic sense of humor. We know he is in heaven now, introducing himself to everyone with a huge smile. We can imagine this is what he said when he entered heaven:

"Hi... my name is Benjamin... but you can call me Ben."

5

The Professor

It is well to give when asked, but it is better to give unasked through understanding.
—Kahlil Gibran

When Dr. Taj Jadavji, one of my former professors, who is also one of the best teachers on how to be a skilled pediatrician, heard about our loss, he reached out.

Taj is a devout and faithful follower of Islam and exemplifies one of the pillars of Islam known as *zakat* (charity).

Ever-so-often—even now ...a few years after Ben died—I see Taj's e-mails show up in my inbox. I always look forward to reading them, because like Ray Matheson, like Rabbi Matusof and like so many others, the lovingawareness energies these great role models exude, with wisdom and compassion, come deep from within their inner being. It comes from a place some call "The Higher Self," "The Deep Self" or "The True Self."

Reading these e-mails by my former professor, convey a profound inner sense of peace and tranquility to me. I do not feel alone. Many caring people have taught me what true compassion looks like in real life as result of my son's passing.

The First Email

Taj's first email to us read like this:

> *"My wife and I were very sad to hear about the sudden death of your son Ben. We pray that his soul rest in eternal peace. We also pray that God give you all courage and strength to bear this tragic loss. I want to meet you in person to express our sincere condolences. Whenever you have time let me know and we will meet for coffee. You will remain in our prayers."*

Taj almost always ends his e-mails with "*You are all in our prayers*" or "*Our prayers are always with you and your family*" or "*I hope your family are safe and healthy and we constantly pray for you.*"

Other Emails

Naturally, there are times when one feels weak and tired as one seeks the best ways to navigate unplanned grief. So often Taj's emails arrive *just* at the right time. They always encourage and they remind. Here are some examples of a professor who to this day teaches me so much about the love of God—many, many years after he taught me how to become a caring pediatrician. Here are some of the words which appeared in Taj's emails to me:

- You are a multitalented person and you have achieved a lot in your life.
- We should have coffee. Let me know if it is possible. (We met for coffee and visited for a long time, talking about things which include, and also transcend our different faith traditions: me as a Christ-follower and Taj as a Muslim).
- We should meet again. Our prayers are with you and your family.
- You are all in our prayers all the time.
- Our prayers are constantly with you.
- Our fasting month started yesterday, and I said special prayers for every human being going through difficult times. I prayed for peace.

We are so much blessed and at times we forget about the suffering of others. May we all be protected from evil forces.

- I hope you are safe and healthy. I hope you are doing well. How is your book coming along? I definitely want to read it when it is published.

Sometimes I share with my former professor how my work as a pediatrician teaches me about the love of God, which not only sustains me, but also those I encounter in my calling.

I Feel Like Crying Now

When I flew to Vancouver last year to run a marathon, a flight attendant came up to me and Corinne. She must have read my pediatric columns in the local newspaper and recognized me. She shared with us about her son who has autism. I was able to encourage her and shared some ideas which gave her hope. Unexpectedly, she said "I am so sorry about your loss." She must have read the column I wrote about what it was like to lose a child—not just as a pediatrician, but also as a father. Apparently, my writings as a parent resonated with her.

Our time was limited because the crew had to get ready for take-off. As she left, she told us, "I feel like crying now. Thanks for supporting me."

Her words landed on my heart. It felt good to bring hope and encouragement to another fellow human being. She spoke from her heart—just like Taj always does, always from the heart.

A man who also wrote from the heart, wrote a book I keep by my bedside. His name is Kahlil Gibran. I mentioned the book earlier. Taj knows how much I respect the author of the book *The Prophet.*

Imagine my joy when Taj sent me a recent email telling me how he visited the Gibran Museum in Lebanon. Taj remembered me. He bought me a key ring at the museum and with the key ring came a quote from Kahlil Gibran:

It is well to give when asked, but it is better to
give unasked through understanding.

When I saw Taj's gift to me, and the Gibran quote, it was clear to me: my mentor Dr. Jadavji gave unasked; not only did he give…he gave with a deep understanding.

Taj helped me understand what it means to be sustained by the love of God.

6

The Teachers

You keep track of all my sorrows. You have collected all my tears in your bottle. You have recorded each one in your book.
—Psalm 56:8

Ben had many amazing teachers. When I think of Bev Thirsk I think of another human being, just like me, but actually wired differently. Different in that Bev is not really a teacher. She is representing the Christ who sent her to teach her many students—each one deeply aware of her caring nature. Her brother is a NASA astronaut, well known in Canada. Bev is very proud of her brother for good reasons. But deep down she is a humble teacher. A servant to her students.

Many of her former students stay in touch with her. The way she models compassion continue to inspire some for the rest of their lives. Bev though her Christ-like example, touches people she never even met herself. It is easy to see why: she *truly* cares. She is kind. She is thoughtful. She is compassionate.

How does she represent the Christ in her? I am not totally sure—we all are partial knowers— but I have a few objects in my home which reminds me about Bev. Mostly written notes.

Notes on January 1

At anniversaries Bev often sends us a written note. I have found that the day of Ben's death is frequently remembered by many—the first day of the year, always a holiday, and always a time when people look back and forward, as we transition from the old to the new. It is one of those days where many remember our family and wonder how we are doing as we count the years since Ben left his body.

In a recent note from Bev, handwritten in the usual perfectly legible writing of a teacher, I read these words which jolted me, because it reminded me who Ben was when he was not with us. This is what Bev wrote to us:

> *"Today I am reflecting on Ben and the time he took to chat with me. It was always a delight to visit with him. I enjoyed the slideshow you created for his service. His fun personality shone through the various activities and his love for family was clear. I am praying for all of you and asking God to meet your individual needs."*

Reading this blessed me. But it also evoked several memories of my son. It made me wonder why Ben could not continue to live and yet he was able to make others feel it was fun to be with him.

At times on the grief journey one can pray, ponder, and pause for answers. There seems to be in all of us a seemingly insatiable yearning to know better; to understand clearly. Three years after Ben left, I have discovered that the *why's* are less frequent when we learn to surrender our loved ones under the care of Him who created them in the first place.

The path to acceptance is never linear. Grief is never linear. It is complicated and often unpredictable. Bev's note was well-intended and helpful. It also created a desire that Ben should have still been alive to do what he did well— not just for his sake, but the sake of those he interacted with.

And yet to cling to our desires, noble as the reasons may seem to be, is delusional. A tragedy in our family was so. It cannot be otherwise. It was my lot. The only way forward I have now discovered, is to cultivate full surrender and acceptance.

Numerous psychologists and mindfulness teachers—Tara Brach in particular, the author of *Radical Acceptance*—always remind us about the importance of cultivating acceptance.

Brach, a Buddhist, wrote very articulately about letting go. We know with our head that clinging to anything and insisting it be different, only creates more suffering.

This Buddhist author has taught me so much, not only about acceptance, but about *radical* acceptance. Acceptance is a bit like fitness in that one continually cultivates it and when triggers unexpectedly arrive, the roots of one's acceptance are tested. The word "radical" means at the root level.

Ben's teacher continues to send us notes around January 1 every year. My own teacher, Alan Cohen, also remembers our family. Three years after Ben died, Alan sent me this email:

> *I know that January 1 marked the anniversary of Ben making his transition. Just to let you know I have been thinking of you and him. I know he is always with you.*
>
> *Much love,*
> *Alan*

The Crystal Bottle

A teacher of Ben's, Ms. Miller, knocked on our door shortly after Ben died. She was one of many teachers who knocked on our front door after they learned of our son's passing.

Ms. Millar gave us a small crystal bottle, from her heart, to remind our family of a verse in Psalms. A verse I have missed, even after thousands of hours of reading scriptures.

Look up Psalm 56 and you will see that it is a mystery. I cannot explain why God does what He does. Why would He want to collect our tears in a bottle? (Psalm 56:8)

I do not know. It is ineffable. But that is what He does. To this day in our living room, we do not have a shrine for Ben, but on a special shelf we keep a space with his watch, his phone, and the crystal bottle inspired by Psalm 56.

The Rugby Jersey

A few months after Ben died, another teacher knocked on our door in the middle of the day. It was Ben's high school teacher and rugby coach. I was not at home at that time.

My wife told me how the teacher delivered a rugby jersey. It was the jersey for the team's upcoming season. Ben of course would not be part of the team.

Inscribed on the back of all the player's jerseys were two letters: BN. It was the team's way to honour Ben by having his initials on the jersey.

Sometimes for very brief moments, I feel directed to open the closed door to Ben's room. All the objects in Ben's room are left as they were the day he died. The only two new objects are the urn containing Ben's ashes, on his desk and the rugby jersey on his bed.

After Ben's funeral one of Ben's coaches, Mr. Gough reminded us how honoured he was to have known Ben, if only for a short time. Mr. Gough wrote:

> *"The reverberations of Ben's passing will be felt in our community for a long time. Ben left a lasting impression that his teammates will not soon forget."*

I was told that the coaches and team wanted us to know that they all will carry the memory of Ben with them in the season ahead—a season which never took place due to the global corona virus pandemic, which unleashed itself a few months after Ben's passing. The collective trauma caused by this virus was unprecedented.

As I mentioned before, my wife to this day, has not set foot in the room where Ben's jersey is left on his bed... a room which we will probably not change for years to come.

Photos and Videos

One of the staff members at Ben's Junior High school sent us an email four days after his passing, sharing condolences. She was exceedingly kind and thoughtful and explained that as the Director of Communications at the school, she knew Ben over a few years, and that it was an honour for her to take all the school pictures of the students.

She wrote:

> *"I have gone through all my photo archives and put together a folder of pictures of Ben. You can access the folder any time. Please call if you have issues."*

Three years after Ben's passing, I can look at photos, but never videos. In videos I can hear his sweet voice and it triggers a deep sense of loss and pain. His voice is so real to me— it is as if he is alive and it was just a bad dream, but of course he is physically gone. Other parents have told me for them it is the exact opposite: when they hear the voice of their departed child, it makes them feel closer to their child.

Real Teachers

We have given away some of Ben's possessions to people who may use it. For example, the old second-hand vehicle which all our kids drove and trained in to get their licences, now serve people in need.

Some material possessions matter to us—mostly for sentimental reasons and for the emotions they evoke. But in giving away non-material lessons we truly give that which lasts a lifetime. Ben's teachers taught us that.

What Ben's teachers gave to us, two parents in need of healing, were lessons embodied in compassion extended from their vast and loving hearts. When I think of their hearts, holding Divine energies similar to the Elements at the Eucharist, a quote by a Christian mystic comes to mind:

> *"The Infinite Love that is the Architect of your heart, has made your heart in such a way that only infinite union with that Infinite Love is enough."*

Bev Thirsk, Mrs. Millar, and Ben's rugby coach all know how to teach. They teach in word and are indeed guided by the Infinite Love who made their hearts kind and compassionate. In my eyes they are servant saints to young people who are sacredly shaped and moulded day by day in these teacher's classrooms.

Like St. Francis, they all teach me about saint –like behavior. They indeed live the famous prayer where St. Francis prayed, "Lord, make me an instrument of Your peace." And later in the same prayer we read, "O Divine Master grant that I may not so much seek to be consoled as to console."

When we give, we receive and one day when these teachers, like Ben, return to be eternally in paradise with their Creator, they will surely hear these words "Welcome my good and faithful servant."

These teachers reminded me and Corinne that we are sustained by the love of God.

7

Honest George

Silence is the language of God: all else is a poor translation.
—Rumi, a Sufi Mystic

It was a quiet Wednesday afternoon in December 2020. I was at home in my study when I heard a gentle knock on our door downstairs. My wife opened the front door, and I heard her say, "Oh hi George, why don't you come in?"

It was not hard for me to recognize George's voice. George has a truly kind and sincere booming voice. His unmistakable, heavy Greek accent makes him the one and only, colorful George. I shall never forget the first time I met him. He reminded me so much of the main actor in the movie *Zorba the Greek.*

Early in my career as a pediatrician, I had a mom who brought her child in to see me and during our visit I mentioned to her that I was planning to get my condominium painted. She encouraged me to get a quote from a painter she highly recommended based on his excellent work ethic. I was surprised when she told me his name: Honest George.

Decades later, and gallons of paint later, and about a year after Ben's death, Honest George was at our door. George was doing his usual annual Christmas rounds of visiting his loyal clients and delivering small Christmas gifts as a way to express his gratitude. That was the purpose of his visit.

Can You Come Down Please?

I was working in the study, finishing off a piece of writing which occupied my mind. I was hoping to only take another minute or two when I heard my wife say "Peter, can you come down please; I need you down here."

I came down the stairs and saw George standing in the dim afternoon sunlight, holding on to his head, his head bowed down as he stared at the ground. I discovered that while I was still in my study, he asked my wife about our family in his usual caring manner. He did not know that Ben passed on. The news shocked him, and all he could do was just stand there without uttering a single word, his one hand holding on to the side of his head. At that moment, my wife felt weak; she needed me to be at her side. Tears were flowing down her cheeks and mine.

I too had no words as I looked into George's deep brown eyes, now filled with tears which trickled down his wrinkled cheeks. It was in the middle of a Covid pandemic and public health officials demanded that we keep at least six feet apart. I did not care at that moment about a devastating virus, viciously attacking our planet and disrupting our daily rhythms. I gave George a hug and told him how much we appreciate all he has done for us over the years and that with God's help, we will get through this awful tragedy of getting used to the fact that our child died.

George just nodded his head, made meaningful eye contact, and slowly turned around. Not a word was spoken. I felt a deep sense of connection—a oneness of three human beings, sobbing together because a child died. The Light in me saw the Light in George. At that moment I saw what other authors meant when they wrote about "Our common humanity."

As he continued his slow-motion walk down our driveway, heading back to his car parked in front of our house, his shoulders were drooping. Deep inside though I could imagine that later he would have felt that his presence and his generosity was the Universe's way to use him to express love to a couple in pain.

A humble painter, the embodied Zorba the Greek, who did not speak a word after he heard about Ben's passing, reminded me and Corinne that we are sustained by the love of God. Needless to say, Honest Georgy will always be our painter as long as he is kept alive by a God who allows him to paint. George that day was more than a painter to us. He was being more than truly helpful.

8

The Donskys and The Smiths

A Muslim, a Jew, a Christian and an Atheist all walk into a coffee shop... and they talk, laugh, drink coffee, and became good friends.
— Dr. Allan Donsky (Psychiatrist and student of Buddhism)

On a bitterly cold Canadian winter day I found myself seated in a coffee shop. My friend Dr. Allan Donsky asked me a penetrating question, "How are your kids these days?" Allan has a dual qualification in pediatrics and psychiatry, and he calls himself a JewBuh—Jewish by birth and very committed to his practice of Buddhist principles. Allan would not kill a fly. As the Buddha taught, Allan always aspires to combine wisdom with compassion.

His question to me came from the center of his wise heart.

I answered, "I am very worried about Ben." I went on to explain how Ben started to cut his arms and how he tried to hang himself at the school he attended one afternoon, following a basketball game. Ben was good at fooling all his peers as the cheerful encourager on the side of the school's basketball team—a position the coach gave Ben, knowing that Ben wanted to be part of the tribe. But at the same time not being able to take part because he lacked the athletic skills to contribute. Ben contributed with his humor, and this humor we later discovered was the smoke screen for his inner pain.

Stuck and Not Moving Forward

Our prayers for Ben's healing went unanswered. Corinne and I felt powerless. We felt stuck. Even though I authored a book about what it means to get unstuck, and how to keep on moving forward -- I had no idea on how to move forward and how to get Ben unstuck from his painful suffering. His depression was like a tight shoe which could not be removed. Each step, each day was painful. Ben was suffering, and as I explained this to Allan, I heard him say after a long pause… "I never do this, but somehow I feel I must see Ben, and try to figure out some options which may help."

Ben had a number of sessions with Allan. On our drives home following the sessions, I discovered it was a good time for Ben and me to talk. I was able to ask Ben some deeper questions. One day Ben shared with me how he found the sessions useful. Corinne and I had reasons for optimism. Allan skillfully did what good psychiatrists do: create an environment for a patient to learn and grow.

Allan did his best and did it with unmatched skills. As a pediatrician, I now understand this about depression: In some ways it is similar to cancer.

Not all patients with cancer respond to radiation and chemotherapy. The best efforts by doctors can fall short. So often we read in obituaries that so-and-so lost their lengthy battle with cancer. Heart attacks can kill at once; cancer and depression, in some cases, do it painfully and very, very slowly.

He Lost His Battle

Ben was brave and fought his depression daily. His amazing life ended in suicide, and he chose that in order to be unfettered by the constraints of his mind and body. Cutting himself gave us our first clue; a failed attempt to end his life by hanging himself was our second clue. The third event at a time of having lost all hope for a better future was the final clue.

Writing Ben's obituary with the help of our friend Janine who is the owner and director of a funeral company, I asked her to say, "Ben committed suicide." I wanted to be honest and avoid the words "he or she died unexpectedly," although I understand people write that because suicide may carry a stigma still in some minds,

Some days I tell others that Ben died by suicide. Even that does not capture what really happened. The truth, that which really happened, and which cannot be put in any other words is that Ben lost his battle with depression. That was his lot. He did not ask to be gifted; it was his lot. He did not ask to be tall; it was his lot. But unlike other depressed teens who do not die by suicide Ben lost his battle with depression.

To this day Allan and I regularly meet for coffee. In fact, mysteriously—or via synchronicity—as I type these words, I got a text from Allan which read:

> *A Muslim, a Jew, a Christian and an Atheist all walk into a coffee shop... and they talk, laugh, drink coffee, and became good friends. It is not a joke. It is what happens when you are not an asshole.*

Michele

Allan calls his wife "Mich" —short for Michele.

Michele and Corinne, both great doctors, worked in the same clinic for many years prior to Ben's passing. In 2013 my wife collapsed and went unconscious. Unexpectedly and coming out of nowhere did I discover her in our study in a state of unconsciousness. It was a shock.

After seeing various professors at the medical school, the diagnosis of a potentially fatal heart condition was made. Her heart suffered from a condition known as paroxysmal supra ventricular tachycardia which if left untreated was fatal. Today a pacemaker and defibrillator in her chest keeps her alive.

It took about five months for this condition to be diagnosed and treated and during that time, when Corinne was not allowed to drive by herself, Michele offered to drive Corinne to the clinic. On days when it was not possible, Corinne used a cab. At the time it was not amusing, but now we look back and laugh at the fact that the majority of cab drivers thought Corinne was not allowed to drive because her license was suspended due to DUI offense.

The very same day Ben died, Allan and Michele were at our door. We hugged; we said very little; we simply experienced what some mystics call oneing.

Oneing refers to the union between us and our Creator, but also the union we experience as human beings when we are on the same page; when we carry each other's burdens; when we sense our interconnectedness; when our deeper selves or higher selves step up and push aside the ego or lower self.

Michele and Allan returned to our home almost every day for weeks. Some days Michele stopped by for a few minutes after work, just to check in on Corinne, always ready to help out and support us to the max.

The area in the basement where Ben ended his life was a mess. I deliberately never wanted to see it. On the night of his passing, I only saw his lifeless legs and did not look around further. Professionals were called to clean it up and later the area had to be renovated.

These professionals did a great job and understandably Corinne and I never went down to see how the renovations were coming along. We simply could not go down into the basement for months following our son's physical departure from this world.

Washed Clean

Michele went down there, and she cleaned up what others never would have thought of offering to do. My other son, Jonathan, told us that many of his clothes got soaked in blood when Ben ended his life in the clothes closet. Michele took these blood-stained garments and washed them in her home.

In the gospels we read how Jesus, the man, taught his disciples how to live like the Christ, the One whose name also means "The Anointed One"

Jesus washed the dirty feet of all his disciples—even the one who was to betray Him. Christ-like examples to this day are all around us. Through those examples we are healed by those who are here only to be enormously helpful. They too "anoint" us with the oil of their deeds.

Jesus washed feet, and our dear friend Michele, washed blood-stained clothes, unselfishly, and showed me and Corinne that we are sustained by the love of God.

Alpha

Corinne and I met the Smiths at our church about two years prior to our child's death. We were asked to be facilitators in the Alpha class. The Smiths were seated at the table we served at. (The Alpha class is a course which originated out of London, England. It is taught globally, and the motive is to provide a non-threatening opportunity to those who want to explore the meaning of life and the role which Christ Jesus possibly can play in a person's life)

After the course we stayed in touch because we sensed a special connection with the Smiths. Billy, a Texas-born meat-loving and forever-Longhorn-football fan is now living in the country where he met his Canadian wife, Karianne.

My coach taught me that we meet people for a reason, a season, or a lifetime. This coach is also a student of *A Course in Miracles* which teaches that there are special relationships and holy relationships. Our relationship with the Smiths went beyond special.

After Ben died, we were visited by the Smiths on a daily basis. Billy texted me often and for months following Ben's passing. The Smiths were one of the few people who stayed in touch on a regular basis—even to this day.

Belonging to a grief group of parents who also lost a child, I often hear some parents wonder why at first many stay in touch and then as the clock ticks, months later, these grieving parents feel forgotten and alone. As a student of human nature, I do not blame anyone for going off the grid. Life happens. People all said the same thing to me—independently over and over, immediately after Ben died.

They all said, "I am so sorry for your loss" and "I cannot imagine what that must be like" and then some said what they thought, while others thought the same thoughts, but did not say it. I am talking about parents who said or thought this *"I hope it does not happen to me because if it happened to you it can happen to me. There is no way I think I can handle such a loss."*

To this day, whenever Karianne calls Corinne, she gently offers her input, her help and whenever else Corinne may need. Billy also sends me a text or calls every so often. Through this compassionate couple we realize how God uses others to sustain us. We continue to be sustained by the Love of God.

9

Many Others

If you asked for a few words of comfort and guidance, I would quickly kneel by your side and offer you a whole book... as a gift.
—Hafiz, mystic and Persian poet.

So much happens in the months following the death of a child. Most of it is a blur—unless one looks at journals and notes made along the way. In this chapter the quote by Hafiz will have specific examples of many people who came alongside us, offering us a whole book of their examples; their gifts to us continue to live on.

I have been privileged to work closely with the American Academy of Pediatrics over a few decades. It is an organization motivated by serving children and their families in the best ways possible and always with excellence and compassion. As a result, this organization attracts top leaders in pediatrics who consider it an honour to selflessly serve.

Martha Middlemist is an example of such a pediatrician. When she heard about Ben's passing, she wrote:

> *"Oh, Peter my heart is breaking for you and your family. Mental illness is unrelenting. I do not have any words to express my sadness at this news. Please let me know of any way I may be able to help you. I am thinking of you and hoping that your family will find some peace... eventually."*

I later discovered that Martha communicated with many of my other friends in the Academy and together they raised funds to have a plaque and to plant a tree at the Academy's headquarters in Chicago in memory of Ben.

A fine pediatrician based out of New York City invited me to talk in New York about mindfulness and preventing burnout. We managed to stay in touch subsequently and when Steve Goldstein, somehow—I do not know how and I never asked— found out in New York about our loss, he told me:

> *"It is hard to know what to say to offer you comfort at this time, but you should know that we are so very sorry for your loss. Ben's obituary was very moving, and I am sorry we did not know him well. We hope your faith, your friends and your family will all help to give you the strength to deal with his loss and that the memory of him will be a blessing to all that knew him."*

While in New York I met a new friend Dr. Warren Seigel, the chairperson of the department of Pediatrics at Coney Island Hospital. Warren also directs the Adolescent medicine section, and as an expert with adolescents he was able to send me and my wife an encouraging note educating us about the minds of adolescents. I never realized how the relationship we build over many years suddenly become so evident at a time of our deep suffering and lost. That insight has helped me rewrite my life in so many ways. Relationships, as my coach taught me, are for a reason, a season, or a lifetime.

I was overwhelmed to hear from various pediatricians all over North America, members of the American Academy of Pediatrics, the Canadian Pediatric Society, and local colleagues.

What amazed me were all the handwritten cards delivered to our home. The ones which really struck me were two cards. Two other pediatricians handwrote these two specific and unusual cards. They were different... different in that these two doctors *both* experienced the loss of a child. They reached out with a deep understanding. I joined them recently at another funeral for a family who lost an adult child. It seems to me that parents who have lost a child cannot help but comfort those who lost a child with the same comfort with which they were comforted.

Dear Friends

I have a number of very dear Jewish friends. A Cantor and his wife who used to live in my city and trusted me with their children as their pediatrician. They too reached out from Toronto. I was told, "We are so saddened to hear of the passing of your precious son. May you be comforted always by the memories you hold dear of him, and may his memory be for a blessing."

At Ben's funeral I was totally surprised how many of my Jewish friends decided to show up in person at a Christian church. One man in particular stood out. I met him about a month before Ben's funeral at a Bar Mitzvah. Sam Fishman told me, "I am very touched by the sincerity of the messages portrayed and know it hit hard on those who themselves might need guidance. Thanks again for the beginning of a new friendship."

When Walter Moscovitz, the obstetrician who delivered Ben, met with me and my wife in the receiving line after Ben's funeral, our eyes met. Neither one of us had a dry eye. Few words needed to be exchanged. Little did we know that a few years later, Walter's wife would make her transition from form to formless and that this dear man, who was there for the deliveries of all four of our children, would face the rest of his future without his Jessie.

At a time of great loss, I always am amazed by the inherently good qualities human beings exhibit. I see it as innate. Later I was allowed to comfort Walter with the same comfort with which I was comforted.

Preparation

A common theme in my life, as I look back, is that of preparation. I was shocked to read about the suicide of Pastor Rick Warren's son Matthew, in 2013. Being a famous Pastor and the author of one of the best-selling books ever, *The Purpose-Driven Life,* made no difference to his destiny. Rick took a six month leave after his son died.

The first messages he taught once he returned to Saddleback, was on the topic of "*How to get through what you are going through*". I followed his teaching online and later ordered the CDs. Little did I know at the time that each and every word shared by Rick, were the words I one day would need after my own son's death.

I asked the Saddleback community for resources on grief from a Christian perspective and was told via an email, "Pastor Rick would love to send you a note of condolence and some resources. Rick is praying for you and praying for how you will use this devastating hurt to help others."

A few days later I received a kind note of encouragement from this man. The death of a child was one thing we both had in common. Rick took the time out of a busy schedule, knowing the pain of losing a child.

Later we received these resources from the ministry:

www.griefshare.org
www.kaywarren.com
www.hope4mentalhealth.com

Attitudinal Healing

I met Trish Ellis a few years prior to Ben's transition. Trish is one of the teachers affiliated with the organization Attitudinal Healing, which has its headquarters in the Bay Area, just north of San Francisco. When we met, Trish had shared with me that she had lost a child.

I felt sorry for Trish when she shared about her loss. Forgive me for repeating the idea that *it is hard to explain the taste of salt to someone who has never tasted salt.* I had no idea prior to Ben's death of the thoughts, feelings and emotions which swirl in a parent's mind and heart after burying a child.

When Trish discovered our news she wrote, "Oh Peter, I am so sorry for your family's great loss. I am holding you all in my heart and know you are surrounded by divine love as you move through the days ahead. Bless Ben on his way home."

Trish notified the founder of Attitudinal Healing, Dr. Gerald Jampolsky. A few weeks later I could hardly believe I was hearing the comforting voices of Dr. Jerry and his dear wife Diane. They took time out of their busy schedules and gave us a personal phone call.

What really stood out about Trish and the Jampolskys, is that they continued to send us notes of encouragement even months later. Trish wrote to me a few days after Ben's funeral, "I hope the celebration of Benjamin's life was healing for all of you." I thanked her for her thoughtfulness and probably the fact that she too lost a child made her acutely aware of the power of her own words.

Dale Carnegie and The Fishers

As a child I was painfully shy and when it came to public speaking I had absolutely zero confidence. When I tell people this—especially people who have seen me do interviews on National and local TV—they always think I am joking.

The pivotal moment I lost my fear of public speaking took place in 1987, when I took the Dale Carnegie training. The training was delivered in our city via the owners of the Carnegie franchise at that time, John and Faye Fisher. I was privileged to be a Carnegie Instructor for close to one decade and was blessed to be able to help others do the same. Since then, John and his best friend Faye—they are head over heels in love five decades after their marriage—have been our friends through thick and thin.

It came as no surprise to find their somber faces at our door the day after Ben died.

We met with them in the same room we sat with the Rabbi and his wife—our living room. As I walked them back to their car, they invited us to join them later for dinner, at a private club in town.

Two months after Ben died, our city was still kept in the icy grip of winter. The wind chill on the night of our dinner caused temperatures to plummet far, far below zero. Sharing a meal in a warm, cozy private room with the Fishers remains, to this day, was a very meaningful moment. They deliberately asked to host us in a private room, knowing that tears would flow unexpectedly. Corinne and I appreciated the privacy.

Ron and Bett

My wife and I met Ron and Bett before we had children. We met in an unusual way. They were put in touch with us because they approached a Christian Family Ministry and asked if they could make a very generous donation. At the time, my wife and I were quite involved with this organization which requested Ron and Bett to meet with us.

When we answered the knock on our door, we expected to meet an older couple who had lots of money and wanted to donate to a noble cause. Instead, there in front of us stood a couple our own age. We immediately became good friends. Together we navigated the vicissitudes of parenting over the decades. When Ron and Bett learned about Ben's passing, they immediately flew up to Canada from California where they lived.

In the days preceding Ben's memorial service, we had little time to spend with them. I was due to run the Houston marathon three weeks into 2020—my 110th marathon.

Given the devastating change in our lives, I decided to not fly to Houston. But after the promptings of friends and people close to me, and upon the suggestion by Ron and Bett, that they wanted to visit with us during the marathon weekend--my wife and I found ourselves on a plane to Texas.

Ron, being an engineer has a sharp eye for detail. Although we were in Houston many times before, Ron and Bett took us to places we never visited in the past. One such place was the Museum District. We felt comforted by our dear friends all throughout the marathon weekend. They extended their kindness and even paid for our tickets to the Lego exhibit.

Ben loved Lego.

As I entered the Lego exhibit, I immediately wondered *What would Ben have said about this?* I suddenly felt an overwhelming feeling of sadness and sorrow. I had to excuse myself and find a private spot to bawl my eyes out and sob until there were no more sobs left.

These unexpected triggers are common in grief. Ask anyone who lost a loved one. They often come from nowhere and are unexpected.

Ron and Bett understood my grief overwhelm me at that moment and offered to leave us at the exhibit alone. But with the help of my dear friends, I managed to face my aversion. I took a deep breath, felt the prayers of my friends who knew I needed it. I dedicated my visit to the Lego exhibit in memory of Ben, knowing deep inside that, although he was not building Lego pieces anymore on this planet, he was in heaven in the loving presence of his Creator.

As I ran my 110th marathon that weekend, I felt the presence of my wife and good friends; but more importantly I felt the wordless presence of the same Creator who made me, Ben, and my whole family--the whole of creation. My marathon of navigating grief had just begun, but as I know we all belong to our Creator, and along the path, spectators will cheer me on. But it was up to me to do the running—one step at a time. Compared to the weariness grief induces, the weariness of completing my 110th marathon was easy.

Apple Pie

A few days after Ben left us, there was a gentle knock at the door. A lady with a kind voice said to my wife, "You do not know me, but I just wanted to deliver a freshly made apple pie which I made for you." Even though the loss of a loved one causes a loss of appetite, we tasted this delicious pie. It was amazing.

Since that day a gentle "stranger" visited us unexpectedly, we have come to know her as Liz. She and her husband, Brian live close to us, and they have had us over at their home a few times. Both have deep spiritual roots and American connections. Of course, we were served Liz's fine apple pies at every visit! We specifically make a point of never discussing American politics. We only discuss that which most Americans can agree upon and a delicious, freshly made apple pie always hits the spot.

The Editor

I have had the honour to write a monthly column on children's health for the Calgary Herald since 1999. My columns usually are sent to the editor in the middle of the month. I was not ready to write anything at this point, and asked the editor if she could use a previous piece and recycle it or if she wanted me to write something new.

Immediately she wrote back and said, "Oh Peter, I am so very sorry. I cannot imagine what you are going through. It breaks my heart. I read his obituary and he sound like a lovely kind boy, only one year older than my son. Please do not think for a minute about the column."

Exactly one month after Ben's funeral, I filed this column to the editor:

DEALING WITH LOSS

Life is difficult. These words are found in the opening line of a book, *"A Road Less Travelled,"* written by Dr. M. Scott Peck.

In the almost 40 years of working with families as a doctor, I have been privileged to walk alongside some families who experienced first-hand what it means to face loss, disappointment, and fear. Life is indeed difficult, and yet beautiful, at the same time.

Researchers compiled a list of stressors in the order of how hard they are to overcome. At the top of the list is the death of a child. This is followed by the death of a spouse, the death of a family member, major financial difficulties, getting fired, a miscarriage, divorce, and marital separation.

Many humans experience these stages after a significant loss: the initial shock, followed by sorrow and struggle and then, as time passes, a sense of adjusting, accepting the inevitable, and in many cases our pain becomes a point of service to others who experienced a similar loss.

Many parents carry guilt, shame, and blame when there is a loss or a disappointment. One of the privileges of being a pediatrician is to walk alongside these heroes of mine and help them see the value of being gentle with themselves. It is not an easy task.

In my medical career, I have never experienced the loss of a teenager to death. But in my own life, my family was given the sudden and unexpected jolt on January 1 of this year when our youngest child, a 16-year-old son, ended his life after losing his brave battle with depression.

Life can be hard but also beautiful. Our family from day one never felt alone or abandoned; we experienced daily kindness and love from our faith community, the medical community, our son's schools, friends, family, and unexpected strangers.

I have done the New York City marathon three times and overall completed 114 marathons. New York, by far, has the most enthusiastic spectators. To be cheered on, literally by millions of people, as one pushes toward the finish line, is quite an experience. And yet, it dawned on me that regardless of the support, in the end it is still the runners' work to get through what they must be going through.

It takes a village to raise a child; it takes a village to bury a child; it takes a village to sustain others when there is loss, disappointment, and fear. I have seen the beauty of that village clearly with 20/20 vision in 2020. Life is difficult, but we are sustained in the "marathon" of raising families together.

***

The PLUS Factor

Philosophers and theologians have argued over centuries whether humans are born kind or evil. Some Christian traditions specialize in making sure the rest of the world never forgets that man is vile and evil and terribly mean, foul, and sinful and of no use whatsoever on their own. One wonders if that line of thinking deliberately ignores the truth expressed in the book of Ecclesiastes which states that God created people to be virtuous, but all followed their own downward path.

When I reflect on how kind and compassionate people were after our loss, I am concluding that all people—regardless of color or creed—are indeed created to be good. In fact, when one reads the creation story in the book of Genesis, it clearly states that after man was created the Creator paused, saw *all* that He had made, and behold, it was *very* good. (See Genesis 1:31; italics added by author)

Certainly, anyone who takes the time and answer this question for themselves has discovered that there are moments –perhaps more so when we see others suffer—when it is clear that the Mr. Rogers' twins, The Rabbis, the Professors, the teachers, the honest Georges, the Donskys and Smiths of this world, The Warrens and Jamposkys, the Fishers, the Rons and Betts and apple pie makers...all coming from various backgrounds... express compassion and kindness from the heart.

All do that, not only because they may have cracked open Sacred Scriptures, or because they may regularly attend a church, mosque, or synagogue; they do it because deep inside they care and that is how they were made to begin with. We all have some moments when we forget to be kind.

These "angels in disguise" do it because inside of them there is a Plus Factor--an inexplicable proclivity to truly care when it matters most. Dr. Norman Vincent Peale, who first introduced me to the concept of the Plus Factor, explains that it comes in many shapes and sizes: sharing material possessions; offering an uplifting word of encouragement; sometimes saying absolutely nothing and giving absolutely nothing other than just being present and radiating a lovingkindness energy. The Plus Factor is indeed a form of Christ-consciousness--far beyond organized religion or cultural faith.

A Franciscan monk, Richard Rohr, reminds us that religion is not to be *transactional,* but rather *transformational.* In his New York Times best-seller, *The Universal Christ,* Rohr explains how everything belongs, how we live in a benevolent universe and how the path of descend is the path to transformation. Compassion is not my truth or our truth; it is THE TRUTH. In the Buddhist tradition compassion is named as one of the four immeasurable qualities. (The other three are love, joy, and peace)

As a student of the Plus Factor, I have had profound experiences of how it is real—the true embodiment of Love, rather than the fear of God being the motive for what some call religion. As Rohr explains so well in his book, real religion is relational and not transactional. Real spirituality transforms.

In previous chapters I shared stories about special people, these "angels in disguise" from various traditions and backgrounds, who when asked for a few words of comfort, would quickly kneel by our side, and offer us a whole book, as a gift.

Our Second Family

Now it is time to introduce the reader to my second family. These are humans who have lost a child—just like me. Many are aware of a communal desire to be free from suffering—just like me. This group consists of people who daily remember the child who died—just like me. When gatherings take place, we always look each other in the eye and see each other's suffering. Without except each person in this "sacred" community of sufferers can look another in the eye and –just like me—simply get it. We understand each other's pain, at times perfectly, and at times imperfectly.

After three years of togetherness, our name has evolved. It started as the "Wednesday Warriors" because we always meet on Wednesdays. Somewhere along the line as we got to know each other better and as we discovered the safe space of our group, things got a bit more relaxed.

As a result, someone in our group started to tell very bad dad jokes, but fortunately for him, the rest in the group forgave him. Others poured a glass of wine—perhaps the one dad's bad dad jokes drove them to that—and our Wednesdays then were known as "Wine Wednesdays."

The current name, Our Second Family, is the name which seems to stick the best. We have become like family.

We all share one single and life-changing event:

--One moment our children were present; and then they were gone—forever absent in physical form.

These are the people who taught me that it is indeed possible to walk each other home—one step at a time; in good times and troubled times. We meet every Wednesday for 90 minutes simply to check in on one another and to support those who need encouragement the most that particular week. Our group has established a loving circle of belonging.

In order to honour their privacy and to avoid a breach of trust, I am not using their full names—only a letter which may represent a first or a last name. I think those in the group may recognize who I wrote about; I doubt strangers will know.

These warriors—people with hearts of pure gold—will understand that though their stories will be shared discretely, the readers of this book may well benefit from reading how we do life together.

These parents, who *together,* are figuring out ways to survive the dark night of the soul, are experts in the field of heart-to-heart resuscitation. They are not philosophers, who give advice or write about navigating loss. They are real moms and dads who try to make sense of their assignment to deal with the death of a child.

I am honoured to be the one chosen to use my pen to share stories of lives re-written after some deep, deep losses and unimaginable tragedies. As I write and reflect upon these stories again, I feel sustained by Love. I feel safe and hopeful. I see the value of cultivating virtues known as the fruit of the Spirit in my own life. These brave people taught me much about being brave. They inspire a warrior mentality even when they agree with the one mom who said, "From now onward every day is going to be shitty; some days will just be less shitty than others."

Olympic Games

Once I shared with the group that I see them as brave. A father tried to argue with me that it is not the parents who are brave, but the children who fought so hard before they died. With all respect to the dad, who clearly was in the initial stages of his grief, I reject such dualistic thinking outright. Why can't it be *both*? Both the parents and the children are brave. There is no need to have an Olympic Games for who is the bravest of the two groups.

There are specific virtues taught to me by my second family. These virtues are love, joy, peace, patience, kindness, goodness, faithfulness, gentleness, and self-control.

I often refer to them as the nine *immeasurable* virtues of true spirituality; they truly are boundless. These virtues are THE TRUTH. Not only *some* truth, but *universal* truths.

10

Love

Whatever the problem may be, Love is always the answer.
—Dr. Gerald Jampolsky (Founder of Attitudinal Healing)

The Important thing is not to think much, but to love much, and do to do whatever best awakens us to love.
—Teresa of Avila

There are so many definitions of love. I like the list given to us, sourced from Scripture, and often read at weddings.

The list describes these qualities: Love is patient; love is kind and gracious; love is not envious or jealous; not proud or boastful; not arrogant, rude or conceited; not selfish; not easily provoked or taking offense; not irritable or resentful; not glad when others go wrong; love overlooks faults and believes the best; love exercises faith in all things and endures without limits; love hopes under all circumstances

It is one thing to read it; it is altogether another thing to *experience* it.

Before I go any further, I must let you know about the man who taught me that when we help one another—-when we love each other—we are actually walking each other home.

This man grew up in a Jewish home. He ended up at Harvard University as a professor and later, perhaps fortuitously, this prestigious institution fired him.

The research he did at the time was not a good fit for Harvard. This man collaborated with Timothy Leary and together they were curious to find out more about how psychedelics impact the human brain—it landed them in hot water. Harvard terminated their careers.

Always curious and searching, Richard Alpert, PhD, headed off to India to look for more. There he met his guru. The guru taught him to love everyone and serve all. Alpert was looking for more than those basic instructions... only to be told over and over by his guru: "Love everyone and feed them."

In a book called, "*Being Ram Dass*" one can read more about the evolution of Richard Alpert, who changed his name to Ram Dass.

On the back cover there are only four lines representing the essence of Ram Dass' guru's teaching. They succinctly capture what Maharaji, also known as Neem Karoli Baba, taught his followers:

—Love everyone.
—Serve everyone.
—Remember God.
—Tell the truth.

The name Ram Dass means "Servant of God." When Ram Dass discovered that a child, named Rachel, was murdered he responded. He wrote the grieving parents a letter. This is what the "Servant of God" told them:

> "Rachel finished her brief work on earth and left the stage in a manner that leaves us who are left behind with a cry of agony in our hearts. As the fragile thread of our faith is dealt with so violently, is anyone strong enough to stay conscious through such teachings as you are receiving? Probably very few. And even they would only have a whisper of equanimity and spacious peace in the midst of the screaming trumpets of their rage, grief, horror, and desolation.
>
> I cannot assuage your pain with any words. Nor should I. For your pain is Rachel's legacy to you. Not that she or I

> would inflict such pain by choice But there it is. And it must burn its purifying way to completion. You may emerge from this ordeal more dead than alive. And then you will understand why the greatest saints, for whom every human being is their child, shoulder an unbearable pain and are called the living dead.
>
> For something within you dies when you bear the unbearable.
>
> And it is only in that dark night of the soul that you are prepared to see as God sees and to love as God loves.
>
> Now is the time to let your grief find expression. Now is the time to sit quietly and speak to Rachel and thank her for being with you these few years, knowing that you will grow in compassion from this experience.
>
> I know that you and she will meet again and again and recognize the many ways in which you have known each other. And when you meet you will, in a flash, know what now is not given to you to know, why this had to be the way it was. The rational mind can never understand what has happened. But your heart if you can keep it open to God will find its own intuitive way.
>
> Rachel came through you to do her work on earth. Now her soul is free and the love you can share with her is invulnerable to the winds of change of time and space. In that deep love include me too."

Ram Dass has taught me that love is always the wise way to respond to whatever appears. My second family has taught me how to embody Dass' wise words. It is my privilege to tell you the truth about this tight-knit group of parents who all share one thing—the unexpected and sudden loss of a child. It is all about how they responded to whatever appeared unexpectedly.

Walking Each Other Home

I met my second family via computer screen, and when it was safe to come out of the forced isolation caused by the Covid-19 pandemic, I met them in person. Although the year 2020 will forever be in my memory as the year that my son Ben died, it also happened to be a year that changed our planet in extreme and dramatic ways.

A virus nobody anticipated, nobody knew much about, and nobody understood from the start, unleashed all hell and chaos on earth. I often wondered how my own son, with his high IQ and his huge empathetic heart, would have navigated the sorry saga of a global pandemic caused by the so-called New Corona Virus. (Some choose to call it "SARS CoV2")

I think of it as the Evil Virus—to live in reverse is evil. It threw many communities into reverse. This virus, in numerous ways, choked off the ability to live life normally. It was evil and foul. The suffering inflicted by this nasty infection upon millions around the planet changed the trajectory of *global* history.

When I think of how human beings are interconnected and how each drop of the ocean adds up to create a wave, and how each wave will forever be part of the bigger ocean—even though it may falsely believe it is a singular and an independent wave—I also realize that what Elie Wiesel said about suffering... is so profoundly true.

Wiesel wrote that human suffering *anywhere* concerns men and women *everywhere*. (Italics added)

As a result of the pandemic, a number of parents who lost a child to suicide prior to Covid-19 were provided resources via Zoom call meetings, because in person meetings were banned by experts. Authorities tried their best to prevent ongoing damage caused by various waves of infections which surprised even the most experienced Public Health bureaucrats.

Our group became a safe place to be fragile; to cry unapologetically and to always arrive at a shared connection—a sense of oneness, though we may have felt alone in the days immediately after the death of a child.

A grief counsellor and social worker led our group of hurting parents with kindness and compassion, with wisdom and warmth, with empathy and insight. All done via Zoom. We met once a week—always at the same time and on the same day of the week. The attendance was always close to

100% because in our desert of grief, our weekly meetings became akin to a weekly oasis where we gathered under the shade of tall palm trees. Every meeting became deep encounters at the heart level.

We felt safe in this community. We carried each other's burdens. There was a deep understanding of how another parent may feel due to the cruel fate thrusted upon all of us. We cried together and agreed that we never would laugh together —ever again. (Later you will see that at some point those who grieve, also learned to laugh again)

When it was safe to be meeting in person, we met for a long walk in nature. One of those walks happened to be one year to the date after our son passed over to the other side. We were noticed by a stranger who passed us and said, "Your group seems to be a very nice group of people; I wish I could join you."

Little did he know why we were such a close group of humans.

The Nicest People You Wish You Never Met

Our grief counsellor, Megan, led several other groups *before* our group and *after* our group. We were told that our group was different. Obviously, each group is different, but what was particularly different about our group is that destiny determined that we were to stick together long after our online sessions expired.

We became like a second family. We still connect every week on Wednesdays—always in love and respect for each other. We speak each other's language. We give each person their space, as needed moment by moment, and adjusting to needs which continuously shift.

As one of the moms in our group observed when she talked to us on Zoom one day, "You are the nicest people I wish I never met." I understand exactly what she meant. When a tragedy strikes suddenly, we wish it never happened, but it did; we had no say in the matter; fate dished out inexplicable mental anguish for reasons we shall never know with any form of certitude...when all of this happened, we had to choose our destiny by how we responded. While we cannot control our lot in life, we hold our own futures in our hands by how we *respond* to misfortune.

We refuse to react; we rather respond; we choose our actions, emotions, and thoughts; we choose who we spend time together with; we choose what

Buddhists call our Sangha; or what other spiritual seekers choose to call "our Satsang;" or what Christians call "our congregation" The power of our decision remains in our hands. We have some agency after our tragedies, even when it does not always feel that way.

Whatever words we choose to describe our "club" or "tribe", our circle of belonging, I know this without any shadow of doubt: love sustains.

In our Wednesday Warrior group, we sustain one another. Nobody is condemned or judged. We may see each other's bodies, but our hearts—that which is inside and cannot be seen-- are vibrationally united on this grief journey. This messy journey feels like we are on a train, and it does not stop anywhere so we cannot get off; sometimes the tunnels of darkness last long; sometimes the noises of the cars straining as they round corners hurt our ears; sometimes one cannot believe this happened. Even a number of years later there are moments when it may still feel surreal to some in our group.

We are indeed trapped on this train, but we are not alone. Love never fails because it is patient and kind. And as The Dalai Lama once said, kindness is his religion. He also said that of all the virtues, patience is the one virtue which seems to matter the most.

Diverse Topics, But Always Walking Each Other Home

Take a recent Zoom meeting. One parent called in from Vancouver, another from Ontario and another from Brazil. Why? Because we belong and we care; we are keen to hear what life is dishing out. What new dung got delivered on the front lawn—unordered and unexpected?

We discussed the upcoming world cup soccer tournament, and one dad who coaches his kid's soccer team weighed in with his confident opinion.

One single mom described the agony of dealing with her dear dog's deteriorating nervous system—a dog destined to deal with a neuro-degenerative condition. The stress on top of dealing with her son's loss was described as "my mental health is taking a beating." What made it worse is that it just so happened to be the dog of her departed son. She shared how she believes that once the dog died, her son and his dog would be re-united again.

A common theme emerged: how to deal with chronic stress and uncertainty. How to deal with the constant drainage of mental energy. We were there for her. We listened more than we dispensed advice.

We then pivoted to arranging our usual Christmas get together. It was only October, but we wanted to make sure we plan far head so that nothing else in December—a busy time for social gatherings—would interfere with us walking each other home.

Another family lost their child to cancer. As a result, the mom ate for emotional reasons and found she stopped exercising. This brave parent realized she needed to get back to the gym and her courage to change the things she could was shared with our group. We all allowed her to explain what it means to be disciplined and to change her exercise and eating habits drastically. We all cheered her on. We were on her side—all the way.

Her insights may help others when she observed that the grief journey drains one's emotions, and to be physically in better shape equips one to deal better with the relentless aversions and emotional roller coaster rides during the aftermath of a child who died.

Some nights before our weekly meetings, I find myself physically and emotionally drained. This recent meeting taught me that once we learn more about the experience of "walking each other home," without failure, a Higher Power, a Plus Factor, a Higher Energy a True Light shows up and floods us with energy. As some of us wait upon this Power we rise like eagles; we walk; we do not get weary. We run together and do not faint.

We discovered what it means to walk each other home, beyond the image these words evoke. (If the words "walking each other home" evoke irritability or boredom in the reader, then it simply means that the depth of these words are not understood—yet. And how could it be understood unless pain gets dropped onto a heart which got pierced, until wisdom arrived?)

We are sustained by Love—even if we do not always know it or have the skill to explain it. A deep knowing arrives—we are not alone. We are sustained—together. So, we trust and serve and love and some remember God and most, grudgingly, tolerate the bad dad jokes I have a habit to tell when things get a bit dark. For example, my wife warned me to stop all my breakfast jokes, or I will be toast. Meanwhile my kids egged me on.

During another recent evening it was not the time to share any jokes. One of the mothers in our close-knit group felt very alone and tired. She admitted that she felt helpless. She did not know what to do any longer to help her young adult "child" who was struggling with addictions and severe depression.

She in all honesty and sincerity told the group, "If there is something that I could do, I would have done it." Later she added that "I would have done more if I knew how to, or if I knew earlier what I know now." We all agreed that few parents truly knew how much their children were suffering.

The usual 90 minutes went by fast. We felt the love, the 'oneing', the caring, and the interconnectedness. Toward the end, the suffering mom told the group she wishes we were physically together so that she could share some "fresh air" with her lady friends ("Fresh air" is a code for some ladies to go outside and smoke cigarettes together).

One of the fathers offered to drive his wife over to the distressed mom so that his wife could smoke with her. We all laughed about this offer which came from his generous heart.

I do not know if the smoking ever took place, but I do know that toward the end of our online meeting there were expressions of gratitude. We reminded one another of how lucky we are to have a group like this; we tried to remember when we started the group; we were amazed that the group was still alive and well. We were even planning our first ever vacation together in Costa Rica. This is the kind of things second families do without second thoughts. We carry each other's burdens; we have each other's backs.

***

In Scriptures we read "God is love." In Wayne Dyer's books we read that the word "God" and "good" have the same roots. Wayne often encouraged his readers that to feel good means to feel God. In other writings we are reminded that we are never more like God than when we love.

In *A Course in Miracles,* we are told that we are as God created us. Many in the New Age community teach that we are like our Source—which means when we love, we represent the Source who sent us into this incarnation to serve and be truly helpful. Christians remind us that we must imitate Christ. As Christ-followers, to be apprenticing under Him, requires that we love like Christ did.

Truth is Never New

My definition of truth is "that which *never* changes." A Universal Truth means that various traditions and denominations and religions all agree on one thing at least: Love.

This truth is never new. It will forever be true.

Syncretism, as I understand it, is when we combine the various religious traditions into one package and place it under a microscope. What do we see? We see various ideas and philosophies, but one *true* energy consistently manifests: lovingkindness, also at times referred to as *lovingawareness*. Unconditionally. Unmeasurably. Sublimely beyond words—ineffably so.

My second family has shown me how to love one another—not in a church or religious institution, but where the rubber meets the road; where real life unfolds; where tears are shed; where parents so often share that the loss of a child is unbearable and that it is hard to even believe it happened. When we join, we join at a soul level; no religion is involved. But we often become aware of the power of compassion and kindness.

We all love and remember our dead children in ways that are hard to put in words.

Shattered or Bruised?

Some people have told me that the death of a child shattered their hearts. My heart is bruised, but not shattered. The reasons for this I will explain in Part III-- with the utmost humility.

I have experienced what it means to say, "I can do all things through Christ Jesus who strengthens me."

When I pass Ben's unchanged room, I remember all the good parts about Ben's life. Little did I know that 2020 vision would teach me that my second family will show me what love means. Little did I know that perception changes everything. That a shift in perception is a miracle. I call it my 20/20 miracle.

I started the chapter quoting Saint Teresa of Avila. She reminded us, and I am paraphrasing here, that it is easy to think too much. Rather than giving in to the tendency to think too much—it seems to be part of human nature after we get thrown into a deep pool of misfortune—Teresa is encouraging us to love much, and to find the best way to wake us up to love.

Such an awakening requires constant mindfulness and daily practice. It is a journey without ending. Our awareness of how love is the answer to all life's problems, will evolve. I shall forever remain grateful that Providence allowed me to walk that journey with fellow parents who are not surprised when I tell them how much I miss Ben and how I wonder what Ben would have done, had he still been alive.

Just today a father in our group told me that when he was at the gym, he saw a teenaged girl who reminded him of his own daughter who died. We spoke each other's language the very moment we talked about how we wonder what our children would have done if they were still alive and with us.

This discovery of my oneness with other grieving parents brought a fresh measure of joy to my weary heart. In the next chapter I will explain how this group reminded me about the difference between joy and happiness.

11

Joy

In Your Presence there is fullness of joy
—Psalm 16:11

Beside my bed I keep two books. My intention is to have these books close by and always visible. These two books are not meant to be left on a shelf. They nourish me before I turn the light off at night. They nourish me when I wake up. They nourish me when I stand next to my bed when dressing for the day ahead.

The Book of Joy and *The Power of Positive Thinking* are the two books I will always keep close by. If forced to keep only two books out of the many books in my home, these classic books will be chosen.

The Book of Joy was written as a result of two good friends who met, simply to share their views on joy—the Dalai Lama and Bishop Desmond Tutu.

Both men suffered greatly-- one under the vile policies of apartheid, and the other escaping from his home in Tibet. The Dalai Lama is now living in India where he congruently lives out Buddhist principles in a joyful manner, being a teacher to the rest of this world.

The Dalai Lama once said that "Optimism is to remain motivated to seek a solution to whatever problems arise." Watch any video of him and one notices how he radiates joy and optimism at all times. His giggles are always infectious.

No Name For New Roles

But how can a group of human beings, parents who share a common pain, find joy and remain motivated by seeking a solution to the problem of a situation which has no name (After the loss of a spouse we are widowed; after the loss of all parents, we are orphaned; after the loss of a child, we are…? *No word exists for such a loss*)

How is it possible that these parents could become open to finding a small measure of joy a few years after we first met via Zoom? During our first few months of meeting, joy was mostly impossible due to a horrible global pandemic on top of the still fresh reality of having lost a child. When we first met there was no happiness, and the topic of joy was never discussed.

Happiness and joy must be distinguished from each other. Far too often these terms are used interchangeably. Happiness depends on circumstances; joy does not.

I specifically remember one of the initial meetings on Zoom. The facilitator led us skillfully. We were discussing if we ever will be able to laugh again. One parent explained that laughing to her will mean a betrayal of her son's legacy and memory. She said, "I will never laugh again." Many in the group echoed that sentiment.

They were all wrong. Very wrong. Time proved them to be wrong and this is how it happened.

Christmas

After things settled down during the later stages of the pandemic, we had more opportunities to meet in person. We walked in nature; we experienced first-hand the healing power of nature. We had picnics and once things really settled down, we met indoors.

One wintry dark night when arctic air unleashed itself over our city, and blizzards pounded the homes we were in, we found ourselves—almost all of us— inside a cozy little home of one of the moms. She is a brave single mom. When she met us at her door, we were also welcomed by a dear friend of hers: a beautiful, healthy Boxer-breed dog, keen to be our friend too. That night G (the dog) became "our" dog.

We gathered for food, wine, and laughter. We exchanged gifts and I pretended to enjoy the silly game where players are allowed to steal each other's gifts (I still am working hard to understand what makes this game fun, but judging by my second family's loud laughter, they had fun— lots of fun.)

And then it hit me in an almost mystical way. It was as if I was having an out-of-body experience where I was not in the room, but I got to watch this group of grieving parents from a distance. I could hear their laughter; I saw their smiling faces; they were not intoxicated; they were simply happy because they were together and being understood. They were in a safe place, not being judged. These dear friends of mine were given a temporary reprieve from suffering. The same people who said they will *never* laugh again were *now* laughing.

Not all parents were present that night. At the time of this writing, I can think of at least one parent who tells us that we are not to use the word "celebrate" in her presence. She decided not to be part of the group that night. Nobody judged her. Grief is messy and it is vastly different for everyone. The mom who has decided to avoid any thoughts of celebration is a dear woman with a kind loving husband. She is still standing—hard as it may be. She is still moving forward, and at times, my wife and I have met alone with this couple. She is an extremely generous human being. This mom may not yet be able to see it, but she practiced at least one of the eight pillars of joy as explained in *The Book of Joy.*

Eight Pillars

The eight pillars are: perspective, humility, humour, acceptance, forgiveness, gratitude, compassion, and generosity.

Some people make fun of the Buddha. I have noticed a pattern that those who know the least about his teachings make the most fun of him. An influential Evangelical pastor, for example, choose to focus on the Buddha's paunch. Often the Buddha is depicted as a fat man sitting in a lotus position. This preacher told his audience, "How can one trust a fat person?" They laughed and lapped up every word of their teacher. Seeing this unfold did not go over well with me as a Christ follower and a physician. I doubt Jesus would have made fun of the Buddha's appearance.

And yet, who can argue with the eight pillars? Who can argue with the Buddha's teaching on the ten perfections which are: be generous, have ethics, know when to let go, seek wisdom, put in the right effort, stay patient, be truthful, persist, be kind and loving and seek equanimity. Equanimity refers to an inner balance and a state of peace *even* in a storm.

Awareness

The mom who has chosen to never celebrate intentionally, and many other parents in my second family may not always be aware of these eight pillars. But I have seen up close how they practice Joy unknowingly at times.

For the rest of this chapter, I would like to continue with more *real* stories which illustrate some of the eight pillars of joy.

Our group is a close-knit group. We are not exclusive, but logically when another story surfaces in the newspaper about a child who died, we feel for the parents. I am about to share a very sad story of the death of a child we never met and parents we never met. We learned about this family's tragedy almost a year after we started to meet as the Wednesday Warriors.

Another Loss

Picture a family who leaves Mexico and moves to Canada. Picture one of the teenagers in the family being depressed. They are in a new country. Resources to help depressed teens in Canada are anemic at best.

One day the father discovers his teenage daughter, lifelessly hanging from a tree in their front yard. She hung herself. She lost her battle with depression. The system failed her; resources where lacking when it was most needed.

Later the father participated in a Zoom meeting which some in our group still attend-- even years after we lost a child. We discovered this sad story and reached out by choosing one of the fathers in our group to deliver a Christmas hamper to the grieving family.

Our group shows compassion; we are grateful we have each other; we appreciate our own perspectives given the time we have had to heal together; we chose generosity; we remain humble by not giving advice unless asked.

Many of us have not yet arrived at acceptance or self-forgiveness. But we are still moving forward—together but at different speeds.

Indeed, not all eight pillars apply in this sad story of death by suicide, but at least *five* pillars were embodied in this story (perspective, humility, gratitude, compassion, and generosity).

Sobbing

One of the moms in our group whose son died from an undiagnosed heart condition, ended up being the "leader" of our group. Her people skills are sky high. Her EQ is obvious. When we first met, she knew about the mental health issues of our children. Issues which killed them when they lost all hope and decided to leave this earth. Her son died from a different cause.

But tonight, she is sobbing. One of her other children now faces mental health challenges and she is scared and tired. She tells us she feels lost and helpless. She cries and apologizes to us for crying. We tell her there is no need to apologize—she is safe with us. She explained that once she was reluctant to talk about her child's mental health issues, fearing it may trigger flashbacks for us. We tell her it is OK. She is with us, and this is a compassionate group. We are here to listen.

Some of our Wednesday Warrior meetings are very social, but tonight it is anything but social. We are in the presence of raw suffering. Some in our group sob with her. I see what solidarity means better than *any* sermon ever preached on solidarity. A mom who is sobbing needs our compassion; our generosity; our humility, our perspective, and as the meeting ends ...we agree that we should be grateful for having this group.

We have not solved the mom's problems as we say goodbye, but at least we have experienced, together, four of the eight pillars of joy. (Compassion, generosity, humility, and perspective)

Unprovoked Attack

One of the moms in our group, L, a single mom, allows G her Boxer dog to sleep in her bed at night. G used to belong to her son who died. It is as if G represents part of L's son and at night when things get dark and lonely.

Having G close by during the darkest nights brings L much comfort and peace.

When our group met at her home, we all fell in love with G—except for the times G polluted the air with some foul-smelling odors which assaulted our nostrils for what seemed to be forever. G specializes in silent farting.

One day L walked in her neighborhood and from nowhere, unprovoked, another vicious dog attacked G and caused much damage. Vet bills were piling up. The owner of the dog who attacked G offered to cover the cost. L felt guilty about that and asked us for some input regarding her latest tribulation.

We shared our perspective, we did so with humility, we followed up with our friend, we offered to hold a space for both—G, the dog and L —we offered to make contributions; one of the mothers offered to come over and take L for a walk, simply to once again be in nature and once again show solidarity.

Again, a few of the pillars of joy applied. (Perspective, humility, acceptance, gratitude, compassion, and generosity.)

Some Pillars Are Missing

Out of the eight pillars you may notice that in various stories two are missing: acceptance and forgiveness. They are missing collectively. They are not missing individually.

When a child dies, I have noticed in myself and in my second family how many of us struggle to accept that it happened. It is so. It cannot be otherwise. It is final. But many refuse to accept that painful reality—at least for the first few years. Sadly, some parents will never be able to accept what happened. In addition, they will also refuse to forgive themselves.

Three years after our children died, we are still wondering what we could have done differently and if it may have had influence. Many carry guilt. One mom justifies her guilt by saying, "As a mom, I am supposed to always provide for and protect all my children. I failed my child and now he is dead." She told me that she is not at all surprised that mothers, more than fathers, are prone to parental guilt.

Grief is a long, drawn-out process. There are no fast-forward buttons. No microwave methods to get to the end "product." For some in the group acceptance may come when they are ready to end their battle with reality and instead fully surrender.

My path toward radical acceptance and surrender is guided by my 20/24 vision to process suffering. As I mentioned previously, in the Book of Proverbs, we read in chapter twenty, verse twenty-four:

"God directs our steps, so why try to understand everything along the way?"

I shall never understand the true causes of our suffering. The smartest theologians, the most articulate authors, the kindest pastors, or priests are at best...only *partial* "knowers."

Since Ben died, I tried for years to understand what happened and why it happened. There comes a point where we must forgive ourselves. If we all knew before our children died what we know now, we indeed may have done things differently. But we did not know then what we know now. As the *Book of Joy* so eloquently tells us, "Forgiveness means to free us from our past." And acceptance is the only place where change can begin.

My second family has shown me the truth of the eight pillars of joy. They have also taught me that to have all eight pillars present all at once is difficult and in some cases impossible. A book with the title of *Radical Acceptance* may not be the right book for some parents who have lost a child. But readers of the book will understand that joy is possible even when imperfection is the raw reality.

God so generously gave me my second family to teach me that I am sustained by the love of God. And as some spiritual teachers teach, love is the way I walk in gratitude.

12

Peace

"I do not think it will be ever possible for me to have peace of mind after I buried my child."
—A Mother who lost her child.

Every morning I cultivate a number of specific habits. Before my son left this planet, I already made it a daily habit to pay attention to the importance of starting each day by setting intentions. These intentions follow a specific and consistent pattern. Over decades it has remained a fixed routine.

First of all—before anything else—I set and intention to be thankful for a heartbeat and my breath. It brings me tremendous peace when I give credit to the Force who made my nails grow while I was asleep, who controlled my breath while I was not awake. I call that Force *my* God. I am also fully aware and accepting that more and more people are uncomfortable with this word and instead they use words such as "The Universe" or "The Divine."

Often—especially in moments where I KNOW that I am sustained by the love of God—I become aware of my many blessings. I see how every good and perfect gift comes from God, my Source. When I use the word "God", I am aware of the risk that some may find it offensive because they do not believe in a Deity.

But as noted at the start, I have decided to write this book from my heart. Maybe the word "God" shall remain a mysterious word. As a spiritual teacher once noted, "From the beginning YHWH let the Jewish people know that no right word would ever contain God's infinite mystery." It is indeed true that there is no word which can contain this infinite and mysterious Force.

I honour my Creator first thing every day—no exceptions. My Source is like the sun which gives energy to its rays. We are rays. We are supposed to be light. Light illuminates and bring warmth. Scriptures refer to Christ as "the True Light" and calls humankind "Children of the light." Given my own experiences, I use the words "God" and "Christ" throughout this book, acknowledging that some readers may prefer other terms on their own quest of seeking peace inside.

Not I, But Us

In his book *The Universal Christ,* Franciscan monk Richard Rohr, refers to scripture where it is said of Christ, "All things came in to being through Him and apart from Him nothing came in to being." (John 1:3) Rohr reminds us that in the beginning God said, Let US make man in our own image. (The word "us" is capitalized, on purpose, to underscore the implications of the presence of more than one Being at the very beginning)

In my own quest to make peace my only goal, I aspire to follow the teachings of Christ. I have chosen to do that specifically— rather than being "married" to the teachings of any church where there is always a risk of humans misconstruing the words of Jesus to suit a church's man-made doctrine. Many of my friends, frown upon Christians fighting Christians. I call that auto-immune religion, caused by a hyper-focused emphasis on dogma and fundamentalism.

I prefer to study the *actual* words uttered by Christ Jesus. I remind myself daily that Jesus was not a Christian; he merely taught life-giving principles; after he died, mankind decided to create Christianity. Words matter. Original words matter and thus, when I lack inner peace, I am curious to learn what Christ taught via Jesus.

For example, in the Gospel of John we read that Jesus said, "Peace I leave with you. My peace I give you. Not as the world gives do I give to you. Let not your heart be troubled; neither let it be afraid."

Let not your heart be troubled or afraid we are told. I cannot get enough of meditating upon those words by the Jewish Rabbi.

Commenting on this soothing scripture, Norman Vincent Peale wrote:

> *Without a deep inner state of quietness, one becomes prey to tension, worry and ill health. A song, a sunset, moonlight, the sea washing on a sandy shore, these administer a healing balm. But they lack power to penetrate the inner recesses of the soul.*
>
> *Profound depth therapy is required to attain healing quietness. A habitual repetition of this one text will, in time, permeate your personality with a complete sense of peace.*
>
> *When tense or restless, sit quietly and allow these words to pass unhindered through your thoughts. Conceive them spreading a healing balm throughout your mind.*

His peace: peace that is different from the peace others (the world) give. A unique peace. Peace that passes understanding. Peace that guards continually— but only if we keep our minds fixed on Him.

I cannot explain this peace with words. Perhaps the Japanese Zen tradition where there is a word for it comes close to explaining peace which passes understanding. The word is *satori.*

It refers to a deep knowing; a certainty; a trust.

Way before my son died, I found the words by Christ and the commentary by Peale helpful. It was as if my life was being prepared for what suffering was to come. My lot was not yet known to me, and yet, without knowing, I cultivated a sense of deep inner peace, not knowing how much I would need it in the days ahead. I will need these reminders probably until my last breath, because losing a child never allows one to get back to normal.

In Buddhism we are told to me more mindful, not just to benefit ourselves but also for the benefit of many others.

The Group's Peace

Losing a child is very *abnormal.* It assaults any decent human being's peace of mind.

As our group continues to meet, I have seen a progression. Although none of us have yet arrived at a total place of acceptance and peace, we at least nudge each other on.

Sometimes a parent will relapse, and we are right there to encourage him or her. By doing this we aim to help such a parent find a bit more inner peace.

The parents who have the most peace never brag or boast about it, but we all aim to comfort one another with some of the comfort we have experienced as we endeavour to make peace with what happened to us.

Sometimes I will share a bit about my own path toward peace, but never in a way that makes others feel they are not there yet. In the end, it is not so much what we hear as what we *experience* that helps us cultivate our own peaceful state of mind.

My second daily intention is centered on the mind. The Buddha explained that all experience is preceded by mind. When we arrived on this planet, made in the image of God, we had no fear in our minds. We were pure and innocent like all babies are. When we left the factory—when we had our original settings-- we were not given a spirit of fear, but rather a spirit of power, love, and a sound mind.

The reality of life shows us that various, inevitable vicissitudes of living will batter us daily, like waves striking the rock at the edge of an ocean. Back and forth. Relentlessly. Without ceasing. From the beginning to the end of our world. Peace then becomes elusive.

It is those moments when I affirm a line I learned from one of my trusted role models, the late Dr. Jerald Jampolsky:

> *The peace of God is my one goal; the aim of all my living; the end I seek, my purpose and my function; while I abide where I am not at home.*

Shalom Means This

The Hebrew word for peace is the word Shalom. This word appears over two hundred times in the Old Testament and its basic meaning is "to be whole, or safe, or sound." Some describe peace as the perfect alignment of body, soul, and spirit. When we experience peace we experience an elevated quality of life.

Given the fact that psychologists tell us that when they look at all the various stressors of living, which losing a child comes in as number one, followed by losing a spouse and then other stressors such as being diagnosed with a serious illness, getting laid off and taking out a mortgage.

How then can anyone in our second family experience peace? Will all of us one day—who knows when—sense that we have more peace than ever before?

I do not have the answers to these tough questions yet, but I have seen how our group, as a safe refuge, provides shelter in the storms of life. I carry an image of us coming alongside the person who does not yet have an umbrella. We hold up our umbrellas to protect that dear friend, a second family member, from the pounding rains. The path toward more frequent peace is paved with patience.

13

Patience

By your patient endurance you will gain your souls
—Jesus of Nazareth (Luke 21:19)

When asked 2600 years ago which virtue is the most important one to cultivate, the Buddha indicated that it is patience.

The dictionary definition of word patience means "to endure under pressure, while staying calm, *accepting* a delay or something annoying, without complaining."

Accepting. Not just accepting, but *radically* accepting. Accepting one's destiny with patience. (The word radical is a word which means at its roots)

In Greek, patience is described as "longsuffering" or "forbearance" The Greek word is *makrothumia*. This word combines the roots *makro,* meaning long, and *thumos,* meaning temper. To be patient means to be long tempered.

The pain of experiencing the death of a child is hard to put into words. The ineffability of this form of suffering, which intensifies after burying a child, and ironically gets *worse* in the second year, is parental pain that is like no other pain. It involves suffering and the suffering is long. It is unspeakable. Yet love endures without limits, patiently... and love hopes under all circumstances, patiently.

In our group I regularly notice how we have remained patient with one another. There may be times when one parent feels particularly weak and thus prone to ranting or complaining. They feel safe to do it in our community because over the years we know that our patience with one another will never run dry.

In one of the most famous chapters in the Bible, also known as the love chapter, we read that the very first quality of love is patience. It is not placed at the top of all the virtues by accident. Patience is indeed a mindset worth cultivating if one were to endure the inevitable traumas of life. But endurance is mentioned toward the end as "Love endures without limit," because all the previous qualities can only be applied if we understand what it means to endure.

As a committed follower of Christ's teachings, I am called to endure, with patience, that which I never expected to encounter; that which I had no say in; that which is out of my control.

Not everyone in our group has the desire to follow the teachings of Christ and yet, I have never felt the group to be impatient with my choice of being a Christ-follower.

In his book *The Mystical Messiah* my coach, Alan Cohen, writes in the introduction: "Jesus Christ has influenced the world more than any other person in human history. Though his feet trod the green hills of Galilee two millennia ago, to this day countless devotees recount his teachings."

I am one of those countless devotees. My motives are the same as those of Saint Francis of Assisi who asked to be made an instrument of His peace.

V's Words Were Haunting

One of the parents in our grief support group, not long ago, drove a rental car in Mexico. He and his wife were sitting in the front, and my wife and I were sitting in the back. On our way to the quaint little town Loreto, nestled next to the Sea of Cortez, we talked about our dead children. I shall never forget V's words as we patiently tried to make sense —three years later-- of our suffering.

V blurted out, "I know shiiiiiit." The S-word was protracted on purpose. He wanted to make sure we all understood that indeed there are times in life when we must accept that we do not know *exactly* why stuff happens the way it happens. As Socrates also said: "The only wisdom is in knowing you know nothing."

It calls for a patient mindset to accept what Socrates said and V's S-word echoed that.

Scriptures tell us that God told the prophet Isaiah that, "My thoughts are not your thoughts; nor are your ways my ways." (Is 55:8)

They say that mysticism implies that some things in life can never be put into words. For some... mysticism involves having a powerful spiritual experience; for others it is feeling of deep communion with God; and for a select few, mysticism involves a profound sense of a shift in consciousness; a change in perception. Mysticism to me means to become increasingly comfortable with the fact that we know incompletely.

The Butterfly's Timing

I had a deeply moving mystical moment in Mexico with V and his wife, A, when they scattered the ashes of their only child who, as V so often explains, "Choose to leave this world"

This dear couple embodies patience in that they patiently wait to be guided as to when or where they are to scatter their daughter's ashes.

It was a pristine day under the deep blue skies, brightened by the warmth of the Mexican sunshine. The tide was low. We walked knee-deep into the Sea of Cortez, a few hundred meters from the sandy shores of Danzante bay.

As soon as A, the mom, scattered her daughter's ashes, a butterfly flew past us. In a week of visiting that area I never saw *one* butterfly. But at the very moment R's ashes landed on the ocean's surface, from nowhere, a butterfly mystically appeared as if to let us know the Universe had our backs. Unless a silkworm dies, a butterfly will not manifest. Some see butterflies as symbolic of new life. A metamorphosis indeed.

At that moment, observing the strength of my dear friends, I sensed that I am not alone and that The Holy Spirit is with me wherever I go on this planet, equipping me to endure with patience.

On my own, I can try to be patient. But it has never worked thus far. And at the age of 67 years, at the time of writing this book, I am more certain than ever that, on my own, I am unable to have the patience needed to endure.

I need help. Help from Above. Divine help. Help only The Holy Spirit can provide.

I will forever admire all the parents in our group who patiently endure their lot day by day by day by day. I can only marvel at their resilience, while I seek to cultivate my own resilience with Help from Above.

14

Kindness

My religion is kindness.
—Dalai Lama

A grief expert, Francis Weller, talks about how we inhabit sacred ground when we grief; how we discover that when sorrow shakes us and breaks us open to deep depths of the soul, we could never even imagine, we learn how to transmit suffering into fertile soil. Weller goes on to add that grief must be communal. Our grief must never be private and hidden from eyes that would restore healing.

If some define true religion as acts of kindness, I was in the presence of religious people, immersed in nature and experiencing what communal grief actually means... *exactly* one year after Ben died.

Because January 1 will always be an important day of the year, many of our friends tend to reach out to our family on that day. Our second family, a few weeks prior to January 1, 2021, reached out to me and Corinne. They simply asked, "What can we do to be with you and to show our support on January 1? We know that was the day Ben choose to leave one year ago."

After our usual back and forth conversation and given the fact that the world was still in the midst of a global pandemic triggered by the Covid-19 virus, we settled on going for a walk in a secluded parcel of land close to a lake and not far from our home.

We were allowed to be outside in bigger groups. Bureaucrats, who were motivated by following procedural correctness, dictated our options. These government officials made up their daily rules, confidently telling us what we were allowed to do or not to do, and our group by now was "trained" to obey well-meaning bureaucrats who were firmly in charge. So, we met in a parking lot prior to setting off for a peaceful walk together.

Because we were not allowed to meet indoors, in a bigger group, and thus met only via Zoom calls, some of the parents in the group were in my physical presence for the first time. One of the mothers in our walking group, whom I shall call O, choose to not be on the Zoom calls. This meant that I never met her in person.

O walked toward me, and as we made meaningful eye contact, she told me, "I have never met Ben, but I feel like I knew him." She was not the first person to have used those exact words. I felt a sense of connection with Ben at that moment, telling him *Ben, I never knew you impacted so many strangers—I am so proud of you, and I miss you daily as you know, but I also realize that the ways I live my life now going forward is the way I shall honour you. May I too leave a healing impression on others, not as a doctor, but also as an author and creator of ideas, using words that are not my own but given to me from Above.*

When a number of people, independently, say the same thing, it seems to me that there is an element of mysticism at work. It is hard to explain and put into words; there is simply a deep knowing that it is not a co-incidence to see certain *recurrent* patterns in life.

Anniversaries

O's husband and I walked together for most of our two hour walk that day under bright blue skies. I shall call him S. The best way to describe S is a human being with a high intelligence as an engineer, but also a father who transformed by his own suffering, always aims to bring hope and calmness to any situation. S is one of those rare human beings who skillfully integrates both his IQ and EQ, on purpose, and always with great compassion and kindness.

S taught me an unbelievably valuable lesson that day. He taught me about anniversaries as we meandered on a path next to the river, which to me symbolized many metaphors of healing, baptism, and the quenching of thirsts in various forms: thirsts for inner peace, for rest, for a deeper understanding. Ultimately all in our group desire the end of a yearning to want things as they might have been. A place to let go and surrender fully seems to remain elusive.

When I asked S how he manages key dates such as a child's birthday, the anniversaries of the child's passing and special days such as Christmas and New Year, he explained that what worked for him is to honour the child *every* day. He added "I see those special days not necessarily as special, but as just another day."

It has been more than three years since we buried our son, and I can attest to the fact that not a single day has passed since that fateful day where we did not remember Ben or missed him and wondered about his presence. The approach of S toward special days has served me well ever since the first anniversary of Ben's passing. It was a radical act of kindness extended to me by a father who, by a mysterious fate, found himself on the path of bereavement.

Over time, S and I have discovered that we think alike very often and that we are similar in our ways of navigating the grief journey. The beauty of our relationship is that although we are not in total agreement about the role of spirituality in our lives, we respect each other; we give each other the needed space; we do not argue or try to convince each other. We simply laugh together, eat together, walk together, and visit often in person or via the phone. Our psychological space is sacred and safe. We can tease each other about him being a carnivore and me being vegan. All of this is rooted in being kind to ourselves and each other.

Our group, even when in grief, continue to radiate energies that strangers pick up.

I Wish I Could Join You

During the walk, where we encountered each other in person and in nature—momentarily free from all the negativity of the pandemic's distasteful disruptions of the rhythms of our lives-- we had about a dozen parents, all walking close by, but not all together at once. Some parents brought their dogs on the walk and younger siblings of the departed children. We laughed and joked around and said hello to smiling strangers who passed us by.

One of these strangers stopped and talked to a mom in our big group. We noticed she was still alone with this man, and so we stopped, waiting for her to catch up with us. One of the fathers in the group teased the mom—a single mom—by saying, "You spent a long time with that guy. What were you talking about?"

N, as I shall call this single mom, told us, "As this guy was passing our group, he stopped and talked to me. He said that our group looks so happy, and he was wondering why and what made so many people walk together. He noticed that the group looked like it was having fun. He even jokingly observed that he may even consider joining us."

N told him, "No... you don't want to be part of this group, because we are all parents who lost a child." We were indeed the nicest people together but the club we joined is a club nobody wants to ever join.

We met for reasons we shall never fully grasp. Against our wills pain fell drop by drop onto our hearts as the poet wrote. None of us are there yet. But meanwhile we extend kindness whenever it is possible—toward ourselves and others.

Not only did our group meet, but years later we are still as close as ever, perhaps kinder than ever, perhaps more compassionate than before, and moulded into people who have the courage to face the demands of the aftermath of a sickening tragedy—together and always with kindness.

The Corvette

One story about kindness which warms my heart was the day a dad, named V, talked to another dad, S, about his new, shinny, fast Corvette. V has his daughter's name, R, on the license plate of this Corvette. It is his way to honour his child who may have loved fast cars.

The conversations ended with V agreeing to pick up S's son at his school. One can only imagine the smile on the son's face when he walked toward his "taxi." Perhaps the son looked around to see if other students noticed. I am sure if they did not see the Corvette, they heard it when V revved the engine and allowed the car to slowly slide forward—until they were out of the school zone and then probably speeding home on a freeway. It was indeed a sparkling day that day for both V, who lost his only child, and for his friend's son, who received V's kindness.

Our lives keep evolving. At times we note all that sparkles around us—nature, friends, laughter, being impressed by handsome waiters when we eat out in fine restaurants, the mothers admiring each other's jewelry, buying a Corvette, "tolerating" some really bad dad jokes by a dad in the group. It is so bad that this father sometimes has to ask his wife to remind him of the punch lines of the jokes.

There is an abiding belief among us that we shall never be alone and that, together, we shall get through what we must get through. Kindness continues to fuel our hearts and minds.

I am reminded of how the Love chapter in I Corinthians 13 ends with "Love hopes under all circumstances." Our deep and intimate knowledge of kindness gives us hope for an uncertain future which keeps evolving. Our lives have become like books that can never be fully written.

15

Goodness

To feel good is to feel God.
—Dr. Wayne Dyer

Imagine a trip to warm, sunny Mexico with your family. Travelling there is exciting. Feel the anticipation. One of your children will celebrate his birthday down there. This particular child was born with a serious heart condition. Surgeries were performed. He is alive thanks to the skilled hands of great surgeons. Thus... the birthday in Mexico is extra special.

One day after his birthday, he feels unwell as he lifts his frail body out of the blue waters of a sparkling pool under the bright, blue Mexican skies. He lies down. Never to wake up again.

That is what happened to my dear friends A and S—two great parents. Parents who consistently bring a uniquely positive energy to all our meetings with their feisty and confident personalities. Both overcame childhood traumas. They were made for each other and then their child died suddenly, in another country, while they were supposed to be a happy family on vacation.

Every year the parents in our group have an opportunity meet with A and S at the gravesite of their son.

A Message From The Skies

A mystical God-moment took place which I shall never forget. It was the goodness of a Power bigger than us. Or maybe it was simply a co-incidence to those who feel there is no God at all? Let us simply say both may be possible. What you are about to read remains a mystery to me. We can never know for sure.

A, the mom, gave all our parents environmentally friendly helium balloons, shaped in the form of a heart. We launched these red balloons all at once, a number of balloons equivalent to the departed son's birthday—if he would have been alive. As the balloons soared, I could still hear A, the mom's sobs. I can picture S her loving husband with his arms around her as they both gazed up to the skies over the cemetery.

But then an amazing event took place.

High above the cemetery all the balloons formed the shape of a huge red heart. There was a message in the calm evening skies over our city. It was as if we were told we are together; we are one; we are loved and that thought we may not realize it co-incidences are ways for the Creator to remain anonymous. The heart in the skies was not a co-incidence in my view. It symbolized that the child who died from a heart condition was *still* carried in our hearts as he soared up to a Higher plane. He will forever be carried in his parents' hearts.

What I appreciate about my second family is not that they strengthen my *beliefs* in the goodness of a Higher Power as much as they allow me to *experience* that goodness. No message from a church can match a deep inner knowing.

I have nothing against churches and institutional faith, except at times, mostly due to traditions, churches can be excessively focused on morals, more than love. The main focus is on dogma and theology. Visitors to some churches feel judged when they should feel included and safe. Being with my friends who care so much for one another is not transactional—it is transforming.

I felt good that evening in the cemetery, only because I experientially grasped what Dr. Dyer tried to say: when we feel good we feel God. We felt safe together as we watched the balloons soar out of our site.

Block Party With Harleys

Two parents in our second family, M and H, honour their daughter by having a block party every year. Streets are closed off, money is raised for a cause (the child died from cancer); celebrities lend a hand; a radio station sends a DJ and occasionally famous professional athletes grace us all with their presence. It is an event I never want to miss. Obviously to support the parents, M and H, but also because the highlight for me every year is a pack of Harley Davidsons.

One can hear the roar of their engines in unison from far aways; the roars get louder and louder. The pack passes the home and then makes a U turn—almost like a squadron of jets flying over a grid-iron football field on an important game day.

But after the U turn the pack comes to a halt in front of the house where this child lived.

The engines are not switched off; they just idle for a while. The long pause seems forever... but because I know what is coming next my eyes get very wet and once my shoulders shook from sobbing.

After the long pause with the engines merely running, the leader of the pack gets off his Harley. He stands in front of his "squadron." They watch him. The wait for the sign—which is his muscular tattooed arm in the air.

And then... they all rev their Harley engines loudly; one roar after another, and as many times as how old the child would have been had she lived.

I always find it hard to video this because, not only does it *always* make me cry; it makes me feel the pain of the parents who bravely have to watch all of this.

To see these rough bikers, show their solidarity in a very compassionate and unique way does more for me than hearing a sermon on goodness. The roars of their Harley engines to mark the years of a life cut short, are like shouts of praise rising toward the skies above.

It is ridiculously hard for me at that moment to buy into the notion as taught by some spiritual seekers that man is evil and vile. I see pure goodness at that moment. I see people from all backgrounds united in solidarity. I am sure Christ sees this too and agrees with God that man was made in their image and what they saw was good. At that moment it is an aversion to me to remember that Luther, when he promoted his theology, called man "a pile of manure."

Humans were made with eternity planted in their hearts, but they were also given a free will, and when goodness is absent, it is because of a free will so often based upon ego rather than love. These bikers have no egos—only goodness and kindness embodied in the roaring engines which bring many of us present at the block party to tears.

More Anniversaries

As one can imagine, the anniversaries of a child's passing can be extremely painful. As I typed these words my phone made a sound to alert me of a text. It is from a father in our family. His name is S. His wife is O. Around now is the time his daughter ended her life, three years ago. Unlike my son Ben, whose life ended immediately after a self-inflicted harmful act, S and O's daughter attempted suicide one day; she remained unconscious and did not die until four days later.

As I read S's text message to me thanking me for remembering to encourage him and his wife, I read his words over and over —for they reflect what every parent of a dead child must endure:

He wrote, *"It is kind of unbelievable typing these words describing your child's death. Who would believe you would have to do this?"*

I was happy to read in his text that he was writing this from Hawaii. It meant that he and his wife took a well-deserved break and elected to spend it in one of the most beautiful parts of our great planet.

This man has become like a brother to me. His goodness toward me is embodied in the story of a Sunday night at an airport.

The Friend at the Airport

I was flying home from Vancouver and had a longer than expected wait of a few hours at the airport. My flight was delayed, not once, not twice but four times. S arrived at the airport from another city and knew I was still there. He searched for my flight, found the gate and at a time when I felt sad for no particular reason, he arrived to visit. We hugged, sat down, and talked about life-- everything *but* the death of our children.

In one of my favorite books on the topic of mysticism, I often read one word used by the author: ineffable. I looked it up just to make sure I understood it properly. The Oxford dictionary describes this word as *too great, or extreme to be expressed or described in words.* "Ineffable" captures the previous words in S's text message to me rather succinctly.

S and I both lost a child. We do not share the same views of God, Christ, the Holy Spirit, or mysticism.

In suffering— as David Kessler wrote so well—there is a sixth stage of grief which is the stage where we can find meaning in the midst of suffering. S has other views. He essentially feels that senseless losses have no meaning. That it will never make any sense. (note to self: Ref to Kessler book)

S and I do agree that at best we all are only *partial* knowers.

I believe that to feel good is to feel God as Wayne Dyer once said. Satori moments reveal that to me—over and over. (Satori is a Japanese word for a *deep* knowing)

To argue over the name God, or the name The Universe, and all the religious dogmas and traditions which separate us, is to miss out on the experience of being sustained when we need goodness—especially after a major catastrophe re-writes our lives... *against* our will.

16

Faithfulness

Health is the greatest gift, contentment the greatest wealth and faithfulness the best relationship.
—Buddha

God is at home. It is me who have gone out for a walk.
—Meister Eckhart

The future of this group and how we will continue to relate to one another is uncertain. At the very beginning it was rare for us to be on a Zoom call and to be asked to share our views, thoughts, and emotions by the facilitator without bawling our eyes out.

I remember looking at my wife, sitting next to me, while we were on a Zoom call with our second family. In front of her lay a big pile of wet Kleenex tissues. Both our tears were contained in that pile. But also, in a bottle in heaven where God mysteriously keep our tears in a bottle.

When our initial official six weeks of therapy ended, it was an *almost* unanimous decision to continue as a group. By this time, we shared a communal desire to move forward together. We somehow understood that to be alone and apart would only delay our further healing.

We were already somewhat healed after 6 weeks—at least we made a start and we wanted to keep going. In the appendix (see back of book) there is a list of what these grieving parents got out of the six weeks of counselling by our two trainers, Tara and Megan.

Only one or two sets of parents, who initially were very much part of the group during the original six weeks of being coached by a team of grief counsellors, needed their own space, and never rejoined our group. Our group understood that various parents grieve in diverse ways. We have never judged other parents who lost a child.

After we formed our final and current group we never had one single disagreement where it led to someone leaving the group and never returning. We have remained faithful to one another —especially during the times when some of us suffered more than others also in other areas of living; the times when an ailing dog had to be put down; or a sibling struggled with addiction or depression; or a demanding job taking a parent out of town on a frequent basis. Through thick and thin we have made sure we have each other's backs. Egos are left at the door.

We have remained faithful first and foremost to the fact that we were given the same task—to live life without our dear children. Our faithfulness in terms of respecting one another and our different ways of coping with grief generates the lifeblood of the group.

When we really needed one another, more so at the beginning, it was not unusual for some folks to call in from distant time zones still faithfully such as Mexico, Hawaii, Brazil, Europe or from "moving" places such as a car, while on a long trip to somewhere else.

We have been faithful at remembering birthdays of parent and anniversaries of the child's death. The latter can be complicated as the next story will illustrate.

Considering the Official Date of Dying

When I connected with a dad in our group regarding the anniversary of the death of his dear daughter, he gently explained that the 5th of the month is when they decided to discontinue life support. M, their daughter, attempted her suicide on the first day of the month and for four days the family hoped against hope that their daughter may survive. She did not. Four days after her attempt to leave, her medical condition did not justify any further life support.

My friend explained that they consider her day of dying not to be the fifth, but the first of that month. I made note of their way of processing what happened and now I faithfully connect with them at the right time. When other parents in our group forget the details of S's daughter's departure, he does not get upset. We are too close and faithful for that to happen.

We all get it that the whole anniversary issue can create many foggy, forgetful moments; every parent is simply trying to cope with their own pain while reaching out to others in our second family. Forgiveness, second chances, empathy, a deep solidarity, all become real in our group. It is not something we know about *intellectually*; we all *experience* it in some way at times when the Universe wants us to learn what it means to remain faithful.

The Table

One of the families in our group lost their only child, a girl named R. R's parents invited our second family and some of R's close friends to have a picnic at their "sacred" spot. We were comforted to know the R's picnic table is located not far from where our second family went for a walk with me and my wife, exactly one year after Ben died.

There were tears of joy and tears of pain. We hugged; we cried together; we were in faithful solidarity with one another. The other name for our second family—the Wednesday Warriors—at that moment seemed to be the most fitting name.

The Future

Will our second family gather at that table, known as R's table for many years to come? Will R's name always be the name on her father's car's license plate? Will we gather by the tombstone in a cemetery and at the same time release environmentally-safe helium balloons into the sky and hope that the balloons will once again form a heart above the grave of a child who died of a heart condition? Will we all go for a walk in the area which was the favorite spot in nature of one of the boys who died from an enlarged heart? Will many of us every year volunteer at a golf tournament which raises money for suicide prevention? Will we attend the block party by the house of the child whose life was cut short by cancer? Will we all await the roar of a pack of Harley Davidson motorcycles who stop and roar in unison... the *exact* number of times that would mark the age of the child if she were still alive?

Will only the mothers in the group go on a weekend "retreat" and get their nails done in a spa, soak together in a hot tub, eat and drink together to the point of becoming wobbly or close to wobbly? Will we all attend dinner at the home of a single mom who invited us to come and say goodbye to the ailing dog who used to be her dear departed son's dog? Will we continue to eat out a nice restaurants and tease one of the single moms when she "pretends" she has a crush on our sexy waiter? Will we attend a movie theatre by invitation of one of the dads, a realtor, in our group who every year invites his clients to a free movie simply to say thanks? Will we hug that dad when he says he does it to honour his son also and then finds himself wiping a tear from his eye apologizing for not being as strong as he intended to be? Will we stay faithful in solidarity with one another for many years to come, even while we are amazed that we lasted this long (three years at the time of this writing)?

It is hard to predict the future as we all discovered in a painful manner. Life is uncertain and as a Buddhist teacher noted, "Anything is possible at any time."

I cannot predict how long the second family will remain close and supportive.

But I can predict, with certainty, that each one in our group will remain faithful to one mindset.

Which mindset would that be?

The mindset that we will forever, to our last days on the planet, remain faithful in honouring *all* parents who lost a child. I am not saying that parents are better than anyone else to faithfully stick together after the loss of a loved one. I am assuming there are also communities to support those who lost a spouse, or parents, or a close friend. But to bury a child is not natural and as a result we need each other supernaturally.

Since it is so unnatural for a parent to bury a child whose life got cut short, I am certain, based on what I learned from my second family, that the faithfulness between parents who lost a child is based on more than mere special relationships. *A Course in Miracles* suggest we can perceive these interactions as "holy relationships."

As the Buddha said, health is the greatest gift, and contentment the greatest wealth. He also added faithfulness as a healing virtue. I can see why that is so. Faithfulness, as I learned via this fine group of humans, is what makes this group so unique and deeply nourishing.

17

Gentleness

"It is all my fault."
—A mother in our Second family

I see a lack of gentleness every day in my busy clinic. I see a mom who blames herself for everything. She says things about herself she would not dare say to her best friend. She is not alone—may other moms do the exact same thing. I have done research on this topic of self-flagellation by moms. I have spent many hours exposing myself to academic gurus on the issue of self-compassion.

I still do not have an answer which satisfies my curiosity or explain to me why so many parents are prone to false guilt.

Doves are often used as symbols for gentleness. Saint Paul wrote in Scriptures, "Be gentle as doves."

I often wear a lapel pin of a dove. It reminds me to be gentle with myself and others. It also reminds me that the Spirit is gentle. The Voice of Love is *always* gentle. Pope Francis reminds us that the Holy Spirit never imposes, but rather *proposes*.

If it is a voice of accusations, blame or pomposity; a voice of smugness or a voice of denunciation, then it is not gentle.

Pretzel theology (man's views being "twisted" to fit their theology) always leaves a foul taste in my mouth when it is not marked by gentleness. It is frequently ego-driven rather than grace-based. Pretzel theology usually fabricates explanations or interpretations which explain how it is fine to go into attack mode and tell others that there is only one truth: *our* exclusive truth. This is not what hurting parents find useful. No wonder some avoid organized religion.

The truth is that many parents of children who die carry guilt for as long as they live. No day passes where a mom or dad may not wonder "what if?"

What If?

What if I took my child's suffering more seriously?
What if I took my child away from his/her environment and we lived away from a toxic culture in some desolate, but safe place?
What if I visited my child more often?
What if I looked at his/her cell phone more often?
What if we prayed harder or longer? What if I combined prayer with fasting?
What if we never had a live-in babysitter and if I stayed at home with the kids?
What if we belonged to a church or what if we did not force religion down our child's throat?
What if I paid closer attention?
What if I was more of a father and less of a coach to my child?
What if I listened to the siblings who knew my child was thinking of suicide?
What if I stayed at home that day when my child chose to leave us?
What if I insisted in the ER that my child be seen by a psychiatrist instead of trusting the doctor who told me I am too worried?

The list is endless. Often these "what ifs?" are also accompanied by "I should have..."

And so, our self-flagellation abounds even more after a child died. One of the fathers in our initial Zoom group, donated his bone marrow to help save the life of his son who had cancer. The transplant did not accomplish what doctors were expecting. The child died. The father blamed himself for "my bad bone marrow."

I am not sure why our group—the Wednesday Warriors—continue to be gentle with each other many years after our children *physically* ceased to live. My theory is that when people have experienced the same pain, they understand each other's suffering that much better.

Our group took another trajectory when we, for reasons I cannot explain, decided to move forward together. With great gentleness these dear, suffering people provide heart-to heart resuscitation to one another.

We each bring various gifts to the group.

So often when a parent engages in false guilt and starts self-flagellating, I as an inveterate encourager remind these parents—similar to what I do with parents in my clinic— to be gentle with themselves.

It does not always work. But the longer we do life together the more obvious it is that my motives are based, not on a false method of trying to give hope, but rather a sincere method of reminding all of us of there is Voice who sustains us. It is the Voice of Love. That voice shall never be silenced. It is eternal. It is infinite.

All we need to do is tune in to the right frequency and listen to the gentle, sweet, non-accusatory voice of Love. —Love which sustains us. This Voice requires us to look carefully with our hearts; we are to listen mindfully and deeply in an unhurried manner. To be mindful means simply to remember to remember. It is so easy to forget that when we are haunted by the inevitable "what ifs" and "if onlys."

18

Self-Control

The first and the best victory is to conquer self.
—Plato

One day your child is alive and the very next day he or she is no longer here next to you. The little cute baby you held in your arms, the same baby who looked at your loving face and beamed a first smile; the child who made you cry when you left him at school for the first time, the teen whose voice got deeper under the influence of testosterone, or the pretty young woman who came to you after her first menstruation for advice...these are now mere memories. They are, as one parent observed, "thoroughly gone."

Never again will you hear that voice of your son; never again will you be asked for advice by your daughter. It is over. And abruptly so. It is so final and so surreal. Writing about this stirs up new emotions in my mind and heart.

Emotions flood every cell of my body. Regulating emotions takes a vast amount of energy and deliberate mindfulness of how to manage aversions.

One may Google the definition of self-control and find out that self-control is defined as "The ability to control oneself, *in particular one's emotions*—especially in difficult times" (italics added by author)

While Googling information on self-control recently, I stumbled upon a quote by Theodore Roosevelt which states that "With self-disciple almost anything is possible."

Does *anything* include managing the unexpected death of a child? Bereavement has become a mountain. Someone in our group mentioned a motivational speaker which boldly proclaimed that, "You can never conquer a mountain; you can only conquer yourself." How useless these platitudes become when one has lost a child. How can self-control make anything possible under these circumstances?

Self-Control via Mindfulness?

Perhaps parents who lost a child used mindfulness meditation long before this sudden sickening tragedy got thrusted upon them. By practicing mindfulness, one may learn about how emotions come and go likes clouds in the sky or boats on a river; how to not fear your fears; how not to believe your thoughts always; how to end the proliferation of thoughts—especially when you are tired and sleep-deprived and thus more vulnerable to emotional dysregulation. Some mindfulness teachers teach that at times unless we control our emotions, we may become prone to aggravating our own suffering.

But it is not always us who caused our own suffering. Destiny determined that a child would die. Why other families had their prayers answered while ours were "ignored" will forever remain a struggle. It will never be fully understood.

In spite of our best practices and intentions, emotions often will proliferate. Of course, mindfulness has tremendous power to reduce or control stress. But there are limits and in severe cases of PTSD, mindfulness can actually make matters worse.

In our group we rarely talk about mindfulness. Some in the group are aware of the benefits, but overall, to the majority it appears to be non-resonant at this time. If we were students then we are not ready yet for the teacher.

Of course, as a doctor and a keen student of mindfulness-based stress reduction I wish I had the skills to "convince" our group about the potential of mindfulness when it comes to regulating emotions skillfully. But in our group we are not into selling ideas or solutions—we may have done that before our children left; now we respect our differences and instead, focus on our common humanity.

A Sad Exception

One of the absolute privileges of being part of our group is to notice that though we are not therapists or certified coaches, though not all of us have a spiritual practice, we seem to innately understand that simply to listen to one another rather than prescribe solutions, is one of the best ways to ensure that our emotions do not kill *even one of us*.

However, there are of course no certainties; no guarantees.

The pain of grief—especially one of the worst forms of grief being the death of an innocent child—lingers. According to scientific studies, only recently did the diagnosis of protracted grief become officially accepted by grief counsellors.

T, a brave mother in our group, went through the relentless wearing down of her own resources. We noticed that her own recovery was slower at times.

As a group, we were always aiming to be there for her. But it seemed that despite our outreach, T encountered blockage after blockage on her path to acceptance and full surrender. She remained deeply troubled by what happened to her. Sometimes she was very much part of the second family; at other times she was alone and distant. In retrospect probably deliberately so.

Before reading further, I encourage the reader to take a break at this time and return later.

***

She looked, but never found. Her restless spirit haunted her daily. We as a group of grieving parents, aware of our common suffering, reached out. We went on long walks together in nature. The mothers in our group spend a weekend at a popular mountain retreat one hour away from where live. The smiling face of T at the spa haunts us all when we see the photos taken during that escape by the mothers in the group. The natural beauty of the Rockies provided inspiration; the bond between these brave women provided strength, briefly, for T. And yet... all of these activities fell short.

What *exactly* delayed her own healing remained a mystery. I suspect she suffered from protracted grief. Her ability to withstand aversion upon aversion wore her down. These aversions coiled themselves around her and squeeze by squeeze suffocated her—similar to the way a python slowly, but surely, destroys its prey.

T struggled for five years after her daughter died. She was brave. T did not make it through her darkest nights. In the end she also lost her own battle with her emotional nightmare. She lost control of her emotions. It became complicated.

It drove her to her death. She decided to leave this world by hanging herself. She chose to leave the same way her daughter did.

We all felt horrible.

As one can imagine, it impacted all of us but especially the mothers in our group. Many wondered if the same thing could happen to them. Some blamed themselves for not being more available. Others blamed the lack of proper mental health care where we live. Timely access to appropriate health care is rare, and even if one wins the jackpot and get the right care, follow-up is often pathetically inadequate. In T's case the follow-up was indeed significantly below par and frankly... pathetic.

Although many moms told our group that T's decision to leave set them back, there was also one father, whom I shall name V. He shared with the group that this new tragedy in our circle of belonging set him back too.

When his only daughter hung herself, it took him years to be able to sleep without a light next to his bed. Now with T's departure he relapsed; it was back to the light at night in order to get some degree of sleep.

If there is one thing to understand about dealing with loss and grief it is this: all of us are incredibly unique and different in how we manage our pain. Yet, each and every parent taught me about some form of bravery and self-control.

Despite this harsh tragedy of losing a mom in our group, we continue to learn from one another when it comes to regulating our emotions not just individually, but also collectively.

Our tight-knit group continues to provide emotional safety. We carry each other's burdens. We experience the face of compassion from close up. In the Hebrew language there is a word *da'ath* and it implies an intimate kind of knowledge involving the whole person and not just the mind.

We all shared the same loss—the death of a child. We all tried to provide heart-to-heart support for one another. We all shared the same experiential knowledge of a very unique kind of suffering. And somehow T was not able to survive her own challenges.

When I see the continued suffering of parents in our second family I am reminded of the words spoken by Mother Teresa when she said when she sees others suffer, she sees their faces disguised as the face of Christ." And as Victor Hugo wrote in Les Miserable "To love another is to see the face of God." These words means so much more to me now. Now that one of my children died.

We all have a communal sense of carrying each other's burdens—perhaps similar to carrying a heavy cross for another when he or she feels weak.

***

As I end Part I of the book, I trust that via the stories of various people who connected with our family after Ben died, the connections of our second family and my connection with you as a reader, there will be an awareness that the human family mysteriously is sustained by a Benevolent Universe, yet free to exercise our own choices for both good and bad.

Obviously, our world is imperfect and will always remain imperfect. That is a truth the Buddha taught over and over in order to help us be realistic.

Imperfection is the norm.

Nobody can argue with that truth. But it is also true that nobody can argue with the stories I shared of how people came alongside me and my wife and the rest of our family during a time of deep suffering. These people made my family's world a bit more perfect and better.

From Stories to Action

As much as these stories are true, it is also true that there will be times in every person's life when they will have to face doubts, fears, loneliness, and despair all by themselves.

Those moments become more intense in the middle of the night; the darkness where we travel alone. We may feel as though we are all alone even though we are never alone because of our metaphysical interconnectedness.

In the middle of long nights there often are moments when the idea of oneness, interconnectedness and community feel like a distant dream. We sense fears and worries. Any belief in us being interconnected gets dwarfed by the disturbing dreams we call nightmares.

In Part II I will endeavour to talk about practical tools which can be put to use in the dark nights of our souls.

These are the nights when we understand that the order we once had is now *forever* gone, and that we entered a dark, silent, winding, long tunnel, named *dis*order.

How we come out on the other side after navigating major disorders depends on so many factors. Many books have brought me tremendous insights, thus providing resilience which enabled me to patiently endure the vicissitudes of learning to live without the physical presence of Ben.

A Book Bono Cannot Put Down

A recent example of such a book is a book written by Richard Rohr. He has taught me much about the process of going from order to disorder and then ultimately... to reorder.

Rohr, in two of his books *Everything Belongs* and *The Universal Christ,* goes into much detail of how the reorder process usually unfolds. The singer Bono refers to Rohr as an author whose books absorbed him so thoroughly that, once he started to read them, it became hard to put a Rohr book down—specifically *The Universal Christ.*

In Part II, I want to explain some of my daily tools which enabled me to deal with my life as a parent who had to bury a child. These are *my* tools which I cannot put down either.

Before we dive into Part II. Allow me to state this unequivocally:

The tools which worked perfectly well for me
are simply my customized tools.

The point of Part II is simple: read it and see if it lands. And if it fails to land, then remember the words of Alan Cohen when he said, "If the train does not stop at your station, it is not your train."

PART II

19

Sustained at 3 A.M.

I am learning a lot about myself being alone.
—Anonymous

Imagine waking up from a deep sleep, and immediately the first thought going through your mind is *"Am I awake or is this a bad dream?"* The clock indicates it is 3 AM. The smart phone confirms it is...really 3 AM. At that very moment you realize there is no human friend to call to help you take the mental anguish away.

The fact that one's child died is very real; this is not a dream. It happened. It is so. It *cannot* be otherwise.

Suddenly, your heart rate starts to climb; there is a knot in your stomach; a wave of nausea arrives and subsides. The room is pitch black. You feel alone. Aversions such as doubt, and restlessness proliferate. Your spouse is there next to you, but the breathing of the person so dear to you—your partner through this ordeal of grief—is shallow and noticeably quiet. You almost wish there were some snoring to indicate more aliveness.

It would be selfish to wake your partner up. So, you sit up and get out of your bed. A sip of water soothes your dry throat. Somehow, you find your way back to your bed and lie there, wondering how a life can be so abruptly shifted from hope to loss; from life to death; from joy to pain; from order to disorder.

Then you remember the eight vicissitudes of life as described by the Buddha (gain and loss; praise and blame; fame and disrepute; pleasure and pain) It seems out of the eight the two which apply are gain and loss. When you have a new child in the family you remember how happy life was then; now you have experienced a senseless loss. What once caused joy now causes pain. It is unimaginable. Taming your monkey mind at 3 A.M. suddenly becomes a major obstacle to peace. This is exhausting. Thoughts continue to proliferate but stop short of overwhelming your being. Somehow, you find your mental brakes and take your foot off the accelerator.

You remember how you read about an angel who told Mary, the mother of Jesus, that she will give birth to the Christ Child, who will bring her *much* joy. But the same child will grow up one day and his dead bloodied body, at the age of 33 years, will be taken from a wooden cross. As his mother, she will cradle Jesus' lifeless, body in her arms before he is taken to a grave. It seems the Buddha's teaching of pleasure and pain apply. What once brought joy now leads to sorrow.

Finally, the words of your Buddhist friend ring true when he told you "I find Buddhism during times of suffering very helpful, because it is something *you do* rather than something you *believe*." So, you *do* something: using your breath to slow down your thoughts seems to reset the results of this rude awakening—for now at least. It gives you something to do. The intentionally protracted out-breathes, in particular, progressively activate the calming part of the central nervous system.

444

At 4:44 AM you are still awake. Another night of insomnia is unfolding, minute by minute. You have only one desire: *If only it were possible to get a break and drift off into some form of sleep.*

The well-known author Dr. Wayne Dyer once said, "Do not get too worried on a night you do not sleep. It is just one night. The next night you will sleep again." How you wish it were true. Instead of focusing on Dyer's oversimplification of insomnia, you wonder about the "co-incidence" of waking at 4:44 A.M. so consistently.

In numerology 444 means an assurance that one is on the right path in life. Seeing those numbers over and over is supposed to clear doubts and encourages perseverance. It is supposed to remind you that strong and caring angles are all around you. Another explanation says that seeing 444 often indicates that miracles are happening *now*. Obstacles are being lifted. Perhaps this is where a shifting of your perceptions may begin?

Is there any proof that this is true? Pain and pleasure are true—you experienced it. Gain and loss are true—you experienced it.

Maybe one day, we will know if all that were said about 444 would be true or not. For now, it makes suspicious cynics frown, while you simply notice the number 444 on clock—on a consistent basis. Once or twice may be a co-incidence, but over and over and over and over?

For now, what is true is that you are alone, and you *alone* can be the one to help yourself move forward.

***

In this section of *Sustained*, I want to look at some ways we can sustain ourselves when we are alone at times. Alone means not being able to connect with another human verbally or physically. And yet *never* truly alone... because the presence of the Creator is infinite and omnipresent.

These methods are very personal to me. I lived through almost four years of grief at the time of authoring this book. What worked for me may not be true for others. But as I mindfully abide in practicing these tools, I am aware of how they are incredibly special in providing a healing balm which permeates my being with a fresh fragrance of faith, love, hope, and joy. They have worked without exception; they sustained me day after day; night after night; week after week.

All Issues Flow From...

In the *Dhammapada*, a book of sayings uttered by the Buddha, we read the first sentence:

> *All experience is preceded by mind,*
> *Led by mind,*
> *Made by mind.*

As we read further, we see that:

Speak or act with a peaceful mind,
And Happiness follows.

A man whom I revere very much, a minister of Christ, a fine pastor, told me he respectfully disagrees with the sayings of the Buddha. He told me everything is preceded by the heart—not the mind. We read in the fourth chapter of Proverbs, a Hebrew book of timeless wisdom, the writings of King Solomon, the King of ancient Israel who succinctly wrote:

Watch over your heart with all diligence.
For from it flows all the issues and springs of life.

Rather than debate this issue, I have decided *both* are true; there has to be a balance between the heart and the mind as Richard Alpert taught.

As I mentioned earlier, Richard Alpert changed his name to Ram Dass later in his life after he learned the universal truth of lovingawareness. Dass went on to become a beloved American spiritual teacher who, to this day, has a following of millions of people all motivated to *love all* human beings unconditionally by finding a healthy balance between the heart and the mind. His practice of Bhakti yoga "infected" millions of spiritual seekers globally.

Given the truth that both our hearts and minds determine the trajectory of all in life and that both matter in terms of us deciding which tools to apply when we go through our trials and tribulations, it thus behooves us to be paying close attention to *both* organs in our bodies.

To ignore the heart by focusing exclusively on the mind may be the more common response –especially among those who become agitated when feelings are brought up. After all, many among us consider the heart as the feeling part of the body while the brain—especially the left brain—is associated with sheer logic and facts. Many influential minds favor logic over emotions because logic is considered more firm, safe, and secure... while emotions are like walking on shaky grounds.

I was not surprised when a good friend of mine, an engineer, who happens to be a keen student of the Bible told me in no uncertain terms that "Scriptures teach we cannot trust our hearts." This friend has an exceptionally high IQ. He is a keen student of apologetics, which is the study of reasoned arguments or writings in justification of certain religious doctrines.

Heart and Mind

A famous Buddhist nun was once asked if she considered mindfulness (the mind) or lovingkindness (the heart) to be the most important. The way the question was framed appeared that she had to choose between the two qualities. Her response was simple and immediate when she answered that *both* are *equally* important.

Scriptures teach that *above* else—that means above any organ in the body—we must guard our heart, not lukewarmly… but with passion and diligence. It may appear that we should see the mind as less important. We can focus on one verse and ignore another verse in Scripture where Christ-followers are actually encouraged to develop the same *mind* as Christ (a Christ consciousness in other words) or where we read "Be transformed by a new *mind*" (Romans12)

I think the Buddhist nun had it right; both the heart and mind matter and scientists have actually discovered there is ample research to prove that a heart-mind connection exists. The research is explained well on the HeartMath program's web site (www.heartmath.com) and also an institute which continues to bless me with fresh insights every week: The Heart-Mind Institute.

Which Clothes to Wear and Which Golf Clubs to Use?

I do not play golf. I have no desire to pay insane amounts of money in order to spend long hours —even when done with one's best friends—walking in nature and spoiling the walk with the challenge of getting a small white ball into a hole somewhere; a hole which cannot even be seen to begin with! Some of my best friends are keen golfers; great golfers; only slightly below the level of PGA players. I am happy for them when they get enthused, just thinking about the game. I cringe when I wonder if they may still be my friends after reading this part of the book!

I always enjoy listening in to their conversations about golf. A lot in sport hinges on our state of mind; our attitude. I once read a whimsical story of a minister who got coached to play better golf. The man was known for his exemplary positive attitude. When he landed in the rough he got all negative. His usual cheerful demeanor vanished like mist in the morning sun.

His coach stopped him and told him to kneel down and grab a blade of grass. The coach reminded the positive-minded minister that the grass in the rough is soft; the clubs are hard; so, it is easy for a hard club to decimate the soft grass and cause the ball to land a few feet away from the hole on the green. The coach observed that, "The rough is only in your mind."

When one wakes up from a deep sleep and thoughts start to proliferate; when it is only 3 A.M. and there is nobody to call —unless you have a close friend in another time zone many hours away—then which tools do you use?

Golfers have certain clubs for certain purposes; we get dressed according to the weather. So, at three in the morning which tools are chosen to be the best "club" to get you onto the green again after you are in the rough? How do you adorn, not merely your body, but your mind and heart, at three in the morning when you feel all alone?

Of course, it may look vastly different for people who figure out ways to navigate losses. There is more than one way to respond after a sudden misfortune. You will read this idea over and over in the book, and it is done on purpose so that it is clear that the ideas I describe are merely ones I have found helpful; *when it comes to grief, there is no one-size-fits-all.*

In the next chapter I want to dive deeper into a method I call the NEST method.

20

Nest

We are what we repeatedly do. Excellence then is not an act, but a habit.
—Aristotle

Approximately four years before our son Ben ended his life and passed over to another dimension, I trained in Hawaii to become a life coach. It was one of the best decisions that I ever made. Alan Cohen, a Holistic life coach, based in Hawaii, provided a training program which continues to thrive and inspire hundreds of his students. Hawaii, being one of the most desired places on the planet to visit and reside in, will forever provide a magnetic attraction to millions around the globe.

Training there then was an easy decision. Given the high quality of Alan's training and having experienced the immense value of tapping into Alan's vast wisdom, I would recommend this training *even* when it was in the middle of a desert, or far away from the natural, pristine beauty of Hawaii.

Alan taught me to think holistically and to always consider the overall, bigger dimensions of wellness. Although Alan's program is heavily weighted toward spiritual living and doing it from a holistic perspective, I have discovered the power of interconnectivity, or what some call "holistic living."

Even as a younger physician, I understood that the body and mind are closely interconnected. Little did I realize that my training in the field of mind-body medicine would lead me to a greater degree of resilience later in my life. This came at a time when I would need it the most, when I entered the dark, long tunnel of grieving the loss of a child.

It is difficult to sustain the marathon of grieving without taking proper care of the body and mind. This requires much discipline. Many parents who navigate the loss of a child are too tired to consistently cultivate four key areas of wellness. I call these four areas the NEST method:

Reflecting on this important topic one day during a run in the mountains, I came up with the acronym of NEST.

- Nutrition
- Exercise
- Sleep
- Technology exposure (also known as screen time)

Nutrition

As a medical doctor who finished medical school in the late 1970's, I have learned a lot since that time. Over the recent years of my long career in medicine, increasingly so, I have learned much about the important role nutrition plays in our lives. It is of cardinal importance and in Latin the word refers to an image of a hinge.

Most doors depend on strong hinges in order to function properly: likewise, our physical and mental health depend a great deal upon healthy nutrition.

When we face aversions and painful emotions, it is common to eat significantly less, get cravings for unhealthy foods, or eat for emotional reasons. Listening in to discussions among mothers who lost a child, some of these moms started to gain some weight after the death of their child; a smaller number found they never regained their original appetite, and some even lost significant weight.

Over the years of immersing myself deeper into the science of nutrition, I have concluded that food, religion, and politics have a lot in common: these topics can become very emotional. Many nutrition gurus hold on to their strong opinions; good friendships are tested because one friend has to tolerate the evangelical zeal of another who, well-meaningly, aim to convert the world to veganism. Fundamentalism does not apply only to religion or politics, but also to nutritional science.

After Ben's death a group of friends understood that making food in the aftermath of losing a child can be hard. These caring people banded together and set up a delivery system to our door where we, on a daily basis had easy access to healthy food—real food, radiating with the energy only found in nature, as opposed to food packed in cardboard boxes and sealed in plastic pouches. The usual stories about all the negatives of eating only a vegan diet did not apply to us for the next six weeks. Since then, my wife and I have enjoyed the pleasures and health benefits of eating a whole-food, plant-based diet. We have no plans to change this healthy habit. We have maintained it for almost four years thus far.

Stories such as healthy food is expensive, preparing healthy meals takes too much time, ingredients are hard to find, and healthy foods go bad too fast have been sold convincingly to millions of people who had good intentions to eat healthier, but then were discouraged by others who told them it is too hard.

In our situation, for six weeks, we ate a vegan style of food consisting of whole grains and lots of plant-based foods. Since the early part of 2020, my wife and I have found that a plant-based diet—some prefer this term over veganism because one can eat French fries and drink Coke and technically call that vegan—is a way for us to keep our bodies healthy and energized.

This works for us, but obviously not for many others. Similar to the grief journey, which is diverse and vastly variable, not all people are able to eliminate animal products which often are quite high in unhealthy, saturated fats. As one dad told me, "If you take meat out of my diet I might as well die," while another observed, "The steak I had for dinner was like velvet in my mouth."

I have experienced the kindness of people who know me well when we plan where to eat out or which restaurant to visit as a group. At a retreat of the men's group that I belong to, the guys who were in charge of cooking remembered that I am a vegan. When we eat away from home our friends now know that eating the vegan way is not just something we tried when food was delivered to our door; it is the way we have consistently fueled our bodies over the past three years. We plan to do the same until it is our turn to transition from this life to the next.

This book is not an academic textbook where an experienced physician shares the scientific proof of the benefits of healthy eating—and specifically as it pertains to veganism. However, when my patients ask me for good resources on how to eat healthy I always mention one website and one book.

The book, *In Defense of Food,* is very simple in delivering this message: eat real food; not too much; mostly plant-based food. By the way, my wife has corrected me many times when I get the summary wrong by saying "eat real food." In my self-defense, real food is food that rots. Food found at some fast-food outlets can be left on counter tops for years and not rot at all. For that reason, I like to insert the word "real."

Regarding the consumption of real food, a useful website which has served hundreds of my patients well is www.prcrm.org

At the time of this writing many children and youth struggle in an unprecedented way with mental imbalances such as anxiety, depression, and inattention. In many cases the chronicity of these mental challenges lead to self-harm. In my clinic I have noticed over and over the brain changes that can take place soon after we provide optimal nutrition to our bodies.

The point of this chapter is that while there will be many moments when the kindness and compassion of other human beings will help us deal better with the tragedies of life, we must be in control of our healthy choices. We are not alone when the helpers arrive as we saw in Part I.

But we are alone when we decide what to eat, how to eat and when to eat. And with the best support possible from others, if we do not fuel our brain properly by eating mostly healthy food, we may not be sustained in an ideal manner. We may even increase our risk of early dementia or premature death and thus deprive our loved ones of our purposeful presence.

Exercising on Ben's Path

On December 16, 2009, I made the decision to run every day for the rest of my life. It is a decision I have never regretted. Ever since that day my quest to run every day has been made possible by a partnership between me and my Creator—I do my part and, by Grace, I have been healthy enough to engage in consecutive-day-running for many years. Hardly a day passes where I fail to thank my Source for favoring me with good health.

Ben died in the early hours of January 1, 2020. The year 2020 was only two hours old when Ben left this planet. I was up all night dealing with the aftermath. Later that day the sun shone brightly, and the eerie quietness of our neighborhood provided me with the best opportunity nature could offer. I was just over eleven years into running daily at that time. I did not run for very long, but I ran with tears running down my cheeks on a very special path where I sense Ben's presence to this day.

I decided to run on a path close to our home; a path I refer to as "Ben's path" because he often walked on that path on his way to buying himself treats—comfort foods which my wife and I reluctantly allowed, knowing it may not have been healthy, but yet, comforting to Ben given his battle with depression. This convenience store is about five hundred meters away from where we live. Since his death I have run back and forth on that path many times, and not once did I "forget" to see the symbolism of my running on a path my son used to take. Running on the path at times caused the triggering of tears.

As time passes... my tears have been replaced by a deep sense of knowing that Ben may not be with us physically, but that forever I shall carry him in my heart—a heart which remains strong enough to enable me to run every day of my life. I plan to use future marathons as fundraisers for preventing suicide and helping those whose marathons are life-long battles with depression. I know Ben will cross with me those future finish lines; I will always carry Ben in my heart. Every day until the end of time.

Heavy Lifting

Another place of exercising has provided me with a metaphor for life. As we age we all have to deal with a condition named sarcopenia. It describes the reality of muscles which become weak automatically as we get older. As much I enjoy running, I *never* enjoyed lifting weights and working out inside a gym...until my wife and I decided to join a gym close to where we live.

The format, known as F45, originated in Australia and consists of 45 minutes of working out at various stations known as "pods" with a group of people —each person doing the same circuit but taking their turns at each pod.

The symbolism of this to me is that we all have similar goals and yet the paths to those goals—be it the goal of inner peace, the goal of handling griefs and sorrows skillfully, the goal of building muscles for heavy lifting moments that will arise—are paths that are quite diverse. At first I marveled at the strength of some of my fellow gym members; now I simply focus on my own goals.

When we started going to the gym we did not know what to expect. Initially it was comically clear to me that I had very little strength in my upper body and my core. Over time I managed to regain some strength by gradually increasing the number of weights and graduating from smaller kettle bells to bigger ones. When I tell the trainers, "I feel different and stronger" it always brings smiles on their faces. As passionate coaches, they experience a sense of purpose and so do I.

The metaphor of starting with the smallest weights, and then making slow but steady progress, can be applied in the ways we establish reorder after disorder; how we decide alone which weights to lift and which weights to leave for later when we are stronger.

We may be in a group of like-minded people, but our free will enables us to choose how fast or slow we want to move forward. The grief journey is just like that.

Sleep

In order to be resilient after the loss of a child or a loved one, we need to replenish and rest. Restorative sleep has been elusive for me ever since the day our son died. I have talked to one of my good friends who also happens to be a sleep medicine specialist. I have tried to wean myself off the use of medications which work well to induce and maintain a restorative sleep.

But three years later I have surrendered to the fact that my sleep will always be limping along. Yes, a tragedy knocked me over and redirected me from a state of order to disorder. Yes, it took a while for me to just lie down. Later, I slowly rose up (resurrected) with Gods infinite power and grace rose up from the "proverbial ashes." Yes, I started to walk again but with a limp. And so, I sleep with a limp for now.

Insomnia is here to stay, and I surrendered to that reality. But I also remember the words from the mystical *Course in Miracles* where we read, "A Miracle is a shift in perception." I now perceive my time of awakening, usually 3 A.M. or 4:44 A.M., as an opportunity to do what the monk Thomas Merton did by reframing the situation as a time to make my bed an altar of prayer.

I have been blessed to learn from ancient Mystics whose deathless presence via their writings speak to my whole being at that early hour of the day when all is dark, and quiet, and we feel alone.

These Mystics stir my heart when I seem to need them the most in the middle of long dark nights. They remind me that it is impossible for a truly spiritual person to be alone by being apart from Love. We are never forgotten; never abandoned; never without hope; never in despair which does not end. An unchanging Force is constantly at work with the same precision as when this Energy ensures that the sun always rises at the exact same spot every day of our lives and that our nails grow when we are fast asleep and thus unconscious of our thoughts and feelings.

When I cannot sleep I always remind myself—I remember to remember—of my constant connectivity with a Spiritual Power we shall never fully comprehend. A very faithful and trustworthy source of energy. A very present Help in times of suffering.

When Saint Paul wrote a letter to a church located in Ephesus he wrote that they he prayed they would "Be grounded and rooted in Love; that you may be able to comprehend with all the saints what is the breath and length height and depth of Love, and you may know the love of (The Eternal) Christ which surpasses all knowledge."

Our finite minds will never be able to comprehend the implications of the love of our Creator who so lavishly sustains us—even when we are unaware—day after day and with a precision far superior to that of the world's most luxurious watches.

In a book written by an unknown Mystic author many centuries ago, *The Cloud of Unknowing and The Book of Privy Counseling,* we read that "Length speaks of God's eternity, breath of His love, height of His power and depth of His wisdom."

So, when I wake up my first thought is to make my bed an altar of prayer. My second thought is to ask Spirit to reveal to me who needs my practice of lovingkindness.

Lovingkindness is a term, also known as *Metta,* and practiced by Buddhist teachers and practitioners. Although I have learned much from my Buddhist friends, I *do not* share their belief that there is no Deity. I wholeheartedly share their belief in *metta.*

To practice metta one identifies the person(s) who may need the prayers or wishes of "May you be happy; may you be safe; may you be healthy and may you be free from suffering."

I have often found that even though I wake up very early in the day after completing these practices to sustain myself, I sometimes drift off to sleep again.

At the time of this writing the practice of Yoga Nidra has been popularized. It does not involve the physical practice of yoga, but rather the methodical visualization of various parts of the body, and thus, through a process of intentional mindfulness, restoring the whole body. Some practitioners claim that the level of restoration is equal to actual sleep. I would agree, based on my own experiences.

Screening Screens

Ben died about three months prior to the arrival of an unprecedented global pandemic known as Covid-19. This pandemic profoundly impacted our screen time habits.

Allow me, speaking here as a very experienced doctor to declare my bias: true science allows for dissenters. Being open-minded means we look at both sides of the coin. I lament the fact that dissenters were vilified during the worst stages of this pandemic. After the dust settled and emotions calmed down these dissenters—some from Stanford University no less—were vindicated. The way it was handled can be debated and *will* be debated for years to come.

What is not debatable is the fact that millions of people, doomed to remain in isolation, and "imprisoned" in their dwellings, resorted to spending more time than ever in front of screens such as TVs, computers, and hand-held computers which on very few occasions actually are used a phone. We refer to these devices as a smart*phone.* (Italics used on purpose to underscore the inappropriateness of the word.) These people ended up not getting infected with Covid...but the sad reality is their minds got terribly infected by useless junk on TV. From millions of TV screens, voices of pundits shouted at maximum volume: "Be sacred. Be very, very sacred."

In my career of almost 45 years as a doctor I have never witnessed such a wave of fear wash over this planet. Many used screens to soothe their fears.

The damage done to our psyche via TV screens and other electronic devices reprogrammed our neuroanatomy and physiology like never before.

Not only did the media stoke fears; it also assisted in the creation of a not-so-subtle-civil-war.

I really believed, two years into the pandemic, that the words "civil war" would be the best way to capture deep divisions. There seems to not be any vaccine to prevent this pernicious default setting of divisions in our current culture.

During those days I continued to serve as a doctor. In the evenings, our home was no different from other dwellings in terms of an increased amount of screen time. But at least our screen time included many movies, rather than toxic politics—movies had the ability to take our minds off the recent tragedy of burying a child, at least for an hour or two at night when Hollywood or Bollywood briefly numbed our mental anguish...and blocked out the hysteria induced by the pandemic. Fear infected many minds—relentlessly in greater numbers than public health officials could comprehend.

The interconnectivity of the NEST method is illustrated in that sitting in front of a TV meant less exercise, more unhealthy snacks, and later bedtimes than usual. Our healthy rhythms were disturbed by our own doing. My mindfulness practice served as a reminder to watch less TV and engage in less social media.

Mindfulness means to be more aware and to remember more skillfully. With this in mind I decided to end my visits to social media sites; to not be on Twitter anymore and to "digest" the civil-war-like drama portrayed in newspapers and political magazine in only small dosages.

The energy absorbed when one follows these debates via screens never served me at all. At the same time, I did not want to do what ostriches do: bury one's head in the sand and pretend all is well.

I have since 2020 determined to screen my screen time more mindfully. In a world where it is becoming abundantly clear that we do not control as much as we think we do. At least the fact that I get to decide my own amount of screen time offers me a secure sense of agency.

It has also helped me discover that rituals, when properly prioritized, and understood, have the potential to connect us to a higher level of functioning; to something bigger than ourselves via a higher consciousness. The results of investing time with good rituals far outweigh the low return of "investing" time and energy into TV shows.

Alternatives to Energy Drainers

I have discovered how rituals serve me well, not just for my sake, but also for the sake of others in that the fruits of my rituals spill over and bring more light and healing to my family, friends, and patients and, hopefully, those who read my books.

The rituals I will explain in the next chapter are my own. I have customized them to fit my contemplative mind and heart. If this were a self-help book, I would have been more forceful and certain to boldly claim that they will work for all. That is what many self-help books seem to do: confidently promise that *one* plan always works for all.

Most truths are partially true. Some are universally true. The rituals you will read about in the next chapter are true for me. How to respond to the loss of a child obviously cannot be the same –even though our situation may be the same.

Of course, you need not go through the same loss, the death of a child, in order to find one or two of the rituals useful in your own journey.

Let us begin by looking at how we end and start our days.

21

Rituals

Ritual is imbued with the Beloved's presence. We need a holy place or thing to awaken us to the holiness of everything. Rituals connect us to something more than ourselves, not just with our intellect, but through our senses, our heart and soul.
—Thomas Merton

How we start and end our days are like bookends. It is hard to say which of the two bookends matter the most. Both are equally important. Bookends hold the books up. Without them, the books may lean over to one side; or fall off the shelf; or look disorganized. To me bookends are metaphors for keeping life together, like my books being neatly kept in place.

Bookends remind me about two key parts in the rhythms of my days: how I begin and end all my days.

Rituals are highly individualized. There are no right or wrong ways to proceed toward the goal of arriving at a radical acceptance of one's lot in life. Since the loss of a child, I have found my customized mourning—and morning-- rituals to be of great value. They fuel me up for the day ahead. They inspire me to move forward –on purpose and in strength, one day at a time. They provide a solid foundation for the days that Grace allows me to love, serve and remember God.

Only "Thank You"

I have cultivated a sequence which served me well over the years. We are told that wise time management has to be congruent with our priorities and values. For this reason, I always start my days, even before I get out of bed, with gratitude. This is a top priority for me. As Meister Eckhart observed, if the only prayer we pray is "Thank You" then we are doing well enough. It is so easy to wake up and fall under the spell of the immediate: my to-do list; showering; getting to work on time; dreading the drive in the blizzard and being stuck in traffic which is always a given when it snows. I use my first few seconds to say my prayer. It is only two words... Thank You.

Unless one cultivates intentional and regular contemplation, the deep meaning of those two words may not be fully grasped. And even when contemplation becomes part of one's morning rhythm, then as Buddhists teach we will always have a beginner's mind—a mind where we may know ninety-nine out of a hundred things, but there will always be more to learn.

The Buddha, said it so well: "Come see for yourself." In other words, start your own day with those two words— "Thank You" — regardless of your circumstances, and notice what happens after a few months doing *only* that upon waking up. Stay open to the shift in perception which may ensue.

Lectio

After I leave my bed, I enter my sacred sanctuary—my "library" — and my space of writing, studying, and meditating. I open any of the Four Gospels where I learn from the words and teachings of Christ. Some students of Scriptures choose to read at a furious pace every day in order to say they read the Holy Book from cover to cover in one year. I used to do that, but after Ben's death, I now practice what is known as Lectio Divina.

This means reading first, then reflecting mindfully and finally... resting in the deep awareness of the Presence. It is a state Eckhart Tolle calls "Beyond the surface layer of Reality."

Tolle often uses two words: "Awareness" and "Consciousness." His purpose is to make his followers more aware of the power of now, by being increasingly fully present. He admits he intentionally avoids the word "God" because as he puts it, "That word comes with baggage."

When I hear the word "God" I am not reminded of baggage and negativity, but rather an incomprehensible Source who has allowed me, through experiential knowledge, to bathe in unbounding infinite love and peace. A deep stillness starts to flow in the midst of chronic chaos, cascades of catastrophes, and uncertainty. My Lectio Divina practice sets the stage for a deep awareness of Presence. I experience a certitude that only Love is real and that which is real can never change—unlike all the other aspects of life where change is certain.

After reading a section of the Gospels, I usually read an inspirational book for at least fifteen minutes. Recently, books written by Christian Mystics who suffered a great deal themselves, resonate with me. Many of these mystics lived 500 to 900 years ago, but their timeless wisdoms, gained via their deep sufferings, remain fresh and still relevant today. Their well-articulated truths have passed the test of time. I have rarely read a single page without experiencing a deep stirring of my heart. Their books will never go out of print.

In his book *The Naked Now,* Richard Rohr writes about ways in which we can learn to see as the Mystics see. Mystical spirituality, and specifically mystical Christianity, is often misunderstood because it is rarely taught. Traditional religion tends to look at it with a great deal of fear and suspicion.

I am very humbled that I have discovered Christian Mystics as role models, teachers and mentors who helped me get through what I have to get through after the loss of a child. (I will talk in more detail about how the writings of the ancient mystics have sustained me on my grief journey, in the final chapter of this book.)

To me, sensing the presence of the Creator long before dawn, and often after a sleepless night, is an ineffable experience. Intimacy with the Almighty has equipped me to stay strong and endure the grief journey moment by moment by moment.

Think of the best intimacy ever with a spouse—physically, mentally and on a soul level. Multiply that by thousands and thousands of times. It is transient at best. Intimacy with my Creator goes beyond temporal bliss; it is infinite and beyond words or thoughts.

Nine Virtues

After the above routine I then pause to review nine key principles which guide me daily. As a practicing and committed follower of Christ, I am always drawn to nine virtues of the Holy Spirit which seem to resonate universally—love, joy, peace, patience, kindness, goodness, faithfulness, gentleness, and self-discipline.

These are the values I want to live by daily. I reflect on them in my library at dawn. To travel on the path of a grief journey without being mindful of these virtues, is like embarking on an unknown road without a map or a GPS. To cultivate these nine virtues, one does not need to subscribe to a religion or belong to a church.

By the way, I have never met an atheist who does *not* desire to have more of those nine qualities in his or her life.

Into Me See

After my sacred readings I pivot to other books. An example of such a book which helps me in the bereavement process is written by one of my most influential teachers. The author of *Love Is The Answer,* Dr. Gerald Jampolsky MD, was the founder of Attitudinal Healing. (see www.attitudinalhealing.org)

Dr. Jampolsky has taught me that the word intimacy can also be sounded out as INTO ME SEE. As I mentioned previously, shortly after Ben chose to leave this world, this kind man reached out via phone to me, a total stranger, thus embodying all of his wisdom and experience and being congruent with what he taught. I thus feel a deep intimacy with his books.

He also reminded me of the twelve principles of Attitudinal healing which now are part of my daily rituals.

Twelve Principles

The legacy of this dear man, captured on a laminated bookmark, is looking back at me as I type these words. His words heal my mind and heart when I read and memorize them, almost daily. It never fails to adjust my attitude-- similar to a chiropractor adjusting a patient's back in order to allow the energetic flow of healing. Indeed, this is what attitudinal healing is all about.

These Twelve Principles of Attitudinal Healing are:

1. The essence of our being is love.
2. Health is inner peace; healing is letting go of fear.
3. Giving and receiving are the same.
4. We can let go of the past and of the future.
5. Now is the only time there is and each instant is for giving.
6. We can learn to love ourselves and others by forgiving rather than judging.
7. We can become love-finders rather than fault-finders.
8. We can choose and direct ourselves to be peaceful inside regardless of what is happening outside.
9. We are students and teachers to each other.
10. We can focus on the whole of life rather than the fragments.
11. Since love is eternal, death need not be viewed as fearful.
12. We can always perceive others as either extending love or giving a call for help.

Before dawn, I allow a Higher Power to see into my core—into me see—and to direct me with abundant wisdom. My inner being, that which many spiritual teachers refer to as "the deeper self," experiences deep nourishment. Some refer to this innerness as "the soul."

It is difficult to put into words what it means to me every time I marvel at this doctor's wisdom. It is indeed a mystical experience. His wisdom always resonates with me—especially the eighth of the twelve principles. (I choose peace inside, regardless of what is happening outside.)

Some days my Higher Power decides to hide for reasons that remain unclear. In the Old Testament book of Isaiah, we read that God hides from us (Isaiah 45)

I cannot remember the name of the author who wrote, "The more we think we understand God, the more God reveals himself as otherwise."

At times of spiritual aridity, it is comforting to review Dr. Jampolsky's practical list.

Journaling new insights in the quiet of the mornings in my writing space, I often only hear the slight scratching of my fountain pen's wide nib over the soft papers of my journals. I also hear the voice of Spirit gently reminding me that I am loved; my family is loved and Ben who left us is loved. I also remember the words by St. Teresa of Avila which talks about, "Let nothing disturb you" and "Everything changes, but God never changes" and "God alone is enough." I have found that to be true. I was chosen to walk through the fires of refinement the past three years. I experienced the true meaning of the word "sustained."

The words of Lou Gehrig, who played for the New York Yankees, "*Today I consider myself the luckiest man on the face of the earth*" echo through my mind.

Also, part of my regular rituals are the words of another New Yorker.

The Father of Positive Thinking

My favorite spiritual teacher is Dr. Norman Vincent Peale, the author of a book which sold over forty million copies, and a book which will never be out of print, because... to this day... it continues to meet the needs of millions globally.

At the time when the book was first published, Peale faced harsh criticism by his peers. Perhaps they were envious that his influential book made him famous when they wanted to be famous too. These harsh critics were never able to reach as many readers as Peale did.

A great number of his fellow Christians were Un-Christlike when they tried to be "witty" by saying that "Peale is appalling while St. Paul is appealing."

Understanding Peale's motives for writing this classic book, such appalling criticism appears to be completely off the mark today. I am deeply grateful that Norman Vincent Peale did not allow his critics to derail his book's purpose. He wrote it unselfishly. His only motive was to be truly helpful. I stand in awe as I contemplate the power of the written word; words first handwritten, on paper in his Manhattan apartment, then assembled and published in over forty languages –thus rippling from New York City to many countries around the globe.

The *Power of Positive Thinking* is the only book which I have read more than one hundred times since I first opened it in 1992. When I read it, I can imagine Dr. Peale's voice reading from his own book—very much like authors reading their own books in an audio version.

I used to read this book at the start of every year; now I read parts of it at the start of most weeks. It equips me to face the almost overwhelming emotions of grief which frequently arise out of nowhere and for no particular reason.

I can hear Dr. Peale telling me to apply ideas which he himself applied; ideas which are rather simple and specific. Ideas which delivered results to millions who purposefully put them into practice.

Ideas such as:

- How to believe in yourself because of Who created you; reminding yourself you are valuable, loved and fearfully and wonderfully made.
- A peaceful mind creates energy; how to learn how to empty your mind from the negative—draining it like a sink—and then filling it up with uplifting thoughts, upleveling to a higher frequency of living stronger than before.
- The power of prayer when the created talk intimately with the Creator.
- Cultivating constant energy, rather than allowing vitality to sag.
- Creating your own happiness.
- How to stop fuming and fretting.
- Breaking the worry habit.
- Creating the power to solve problems.
- Relaxing for easy power.
- Finding the right prescription for managing sorrows and heartaches.
- Learning to draw upon that Higher Power.

The emotions evoked by grief and other losses always lurk in the dark; they may surface with no warning. At times like these, it is indeed reassuring to have a method which, as Peale wrote, "lubricates the mind and provides a healing balm which spreads throughout one's being."

I can visualize that healing balm soothing my heart, which to this day, hurts as I walk past the room where Ben once did his homework, slept in on weekends and connected with his friends via his well-used cell phone.

Other Teachers and Soul Coaches

Following gratitude, Lectio Divina, journaling, time in being taught by the Mystical Messiah, reminders from perennial bestselling authors, I then make it my practice to review some of the ideas I "discovered" serendipitously. Could it also be that these ideas discovered me through an unseen Force, desiring that as gift to His beloved?

Through books and podcasts, thousands of hours later, I have found the benefits of learning by association. A pivotal example is a recent podcast which profoundly changed my perceptions. The podcast, *Another Name for Every Thing,* taught me about the Cosmic Egg. This is my illustration of an idea or image which, serendipitously, raised my level of consciousness.

Imagine an egg. In the center is the yolk. The yolk represents ***My** Story*; it is the story about my pain, my pleasures, my family, and my work; my ideas about life. Obviously, this may vary greatly from person to person, and that is why I make the word "My" bold. We all know that life's ups and downs mold us to come up with our own narratives about ourselves or the situations we may experience.

Around the yolk is egg white. This represents ***Our** Story.* Our story is about *our* tribe or *our* community. For some religious types it may represent their denomination or tradition. Some students of *A Course in Miracles* gather online, and as a global community, learn from one another. They may talk about their story, but often in the context of their story being a bigger story. It is still not ***The*** Story. It is more like a specific church community with beliefs that are not always universal. The requirement of ***The** Story* is that it be universally true.

The third part of the Cosmic egg is the part which intrigued me the most. This is the part surrounding the egg yolk, and the egg white. It is known as *The Story***.** This is what I call the absolute bigger truths—far above personal stories or tribal stories. Some refer to this also as the "Universal Story."

An example would be ethics which do not exclusively belong to any specific tradition or religion. Christians do not have a monopoly on virtues such as not killing, not stealing, not telling lies, and respecting life. Buddhists teach the same. As Richard Rohr said it so well, "There is no Christian, Muslim, Jewish or Hindu way to run a soup kitchen."

Buddhist teacher, Joseph Goldstein, teaches that Buddhism is not only a path to wisdom and concentration. It also is a path where everything *primarily* hinges on ethics or virtues.

Mindfulness

Every day, as part of my morning rituals, I practice Vipassana mindfulness meditations. I have three favorite mindfulness teachers: Joseph Goldstein a Buddhist teacher, James Finley a Christian mystic, and Jon Kabat-Zinn an academic clinician, known for his work in advocating for mindfulness-based stress reduction. (MBSR is taught globally today because of the pioneering work of Kabat-Zinn)

James Finley, writing about Christian meditation and mindfulness says that "It draws us into a wordless awareness of oneness with God beyond what thoughts can grasp or words can adequately convey." (15)

He goes on to add that meditation requires us to become willing to be even *more* perplexed. "We must be willing to befriend our perplexity as a way of dying to our futile efforts to grasp the ungraspable depths that meditation invites us to discover." (See *Christian Meditation; experiencing the Presence of God* Harper One Publishers; 2004)

Jon Kabat-Zinn defines mindfulness as paying attention, on purpose, without any judgment and doing so moment by moment. As I am writing these words I am noting Jon's book next to me—*Wherever You Go, There You Are.* This book has equipped my mental muscles to stay present and strong when I face what the famous American psychologist Abraham Maslow calls "worthwhile suffering." Navigating the aftermath of the loss of a child is a tough experience. Is the suffering really worthwhile? Maslow would say yes.

Since I had no choice in the matter—it was thrusted upon me and my wife—I can attest to the accuracy of Maslow's words, because what has not broken me has made me stronger. It is by abiding ardently that I have learned the fact that, though my environment cannot be changed, I can change. As Kabat-Zinn writes, wherever we go there we are— either mindfully or sleepwalking.

Joseph Goldstein in his book *Mindfulness,* explains the four pillars of being mindful, as taught by the Buddhist tradition. The first pillar deals with being mindful of the body and using the breath as an anchor. The beautiful aspects of using the breath to manage stress and fears in the middle of the night, or at any other time, is that it is so simple; it can be done anywhere and anytime. And as a medical doctor motivated to share tools which are rooted in solid scientific research I find it *not* surprising when psychologists tell us that 50% of all anxieties can be significantly controlled and reduced by the practice of mindful breathing.

Mindfulness has helped me to see things in a new light. To me the word insight means to be aligned with Light. My beginner's mind offers me fresh insights, like streetlights, along the road called "bereavement." My shifts in perceptions allow me to see things in a new light.

Best Places to Search.

When I mention seeing "in a new light" I am reminded of a Sufi tale. (Sufism is a mystical tradition in the Muslim faith).

Once upon a time a Sufi master lost the key to his house. He got on his knees and hands and started running his fingers through every blade of grass. A few moments later some of the Master's students saw him, came over and asked him, "Master what is wrong?" The Master answered, "I lost the key to my house."

Soon the Master and his students were all on the grass looking for the lost key to his house. Over time the sun got hotter and hotter. One of the students asked the Master, "Have you any idea where you might have lost the key?"

The Master replied "Of course. I lost it in the house. His students were surprised and wanted to know from the Master why then were they all looking for the lost key outside the house, to which the Master replied, "Isn't it obvious? There is more light here."

All of us at times search for explanations and truth, or for what we *think* we lost. We are sure of our motives. But are we looking in the right place?

Renewing of the Mind

In my own case I trusted that as long as I sought after proper medical care for our son and trusted God to heal him from depression, he will once day grow up and use his God-given high IQ to serve all God's children in whatever way Destiny guided him. I have learned to let go of my certitude.

As I said in the introduction of this book, my idea of perfect vison being 20/20 in the year 2020 turned out to be *quite* different. I cannot claim to understand why suffering was allowed to befall us. But with certain vision, vison which becomes clearer daily when I contemplate the mystery of suffering, I can confirm grief has not destroyed me; neither does it define me. It has developed me. I may find myself in the cloud of the unknowing, but the Divine peace emanating from my Source sustains me daily. It passes understanding. It guards my mind and heart.

As mentioned before, I belong to a gym where my wife and I have seen the physical value of daily workouts. As we age, we gradually lose our muscle mass—about a quarter pound per year starting at age forty. Many older people fall and never recover after a broken hip. That is the physical realm.

Losing a child *almost* made my wife and I *not* rise up after a mental fall. Our mental muscles were weak and fatigued.

In addition to faith muscles, my mental muscles have been developed early every morning through practicing rituals such as Vipassana meditation, also known as Insight meditation. It has become one of the best places to search—not like the Sufi story but rather search where there is true Light.

By Grace, the value of mental muscle cultivation exercises in the form of mindfulness sustained me day by day. Without exception, daily mindfulness meditation continues to serve me perfectly well. It is in our quiescent states that we learn to skillfully move forward daily. Moments of knowing and experiencing true peace and spiritual comfort early in the day sets the tone for the rest of the day. I am convinced of the truth contained in these wise words written by a Scottish essayist, historian, and philosopher, born in 1795, and who died in London in 1881.

Thomas Carlyle said, "Silence is the element in which great things fashion themselves."

Music

There is a time to be silent and then there is a time for music in my daily patterns of building resilience. It has been said that where words fail, music speaks. Or as Pablo Casals noted, "Music is the divine way to tell beautiful, poetic things to the heart."

Celine Dion and Andrea Bocelli are famous for a duet they sang: *The Prayer.* The lyrics and the melody both speak to my *whole* being some mornings—either in my study or during a run in nature.

We are reminded in the song, and I am paraphrasing here, that we ask to be watched, guided and helped wherever we go; that at times when we do not know, we may be led to a safe place and be guided by grace; we pray that life be kind and that each soul will find another soul to love. Like every child, we hope to find a place to experience safety and the faith to believe that it will be possible.

In 1990 my wife and I spent our honeymoon on the Caribbean island of Antigua. One Sunday afternoon we did the thing that many tourists do: attend a steel band concert on a mountain top with a stunning view of an old harbor below.

While there, my always-observant wife spotted two men standing not far away from us. They stood by themselves. One of the men was Eric Clapton. I observed how they were totally captured by the music. They were oblivious of people surrounding them; people who glanced every once in a while in Clapton's direction.

Two weeks later we heard the news that Clapton's son passed away. At that time, the sad news was just that —sad news. And as is the case so often, we briefly feel sorry for another person, and then move on with our own life.

Today the words of Eric Clapton's famous song "*Tears in Heaven*" mean so much more to me now. My wife, on the other hand, cannot listen to the song. It always stirs up raw emotions inside her grieving heart. I find Clapton's song deeply comforting-- even though it is rather sad and soulful to the core.

I love the soul-stirring lyrics. It reminds me of what many parents ask after losing a child. Will you know my name when I see you in heaven? Will you hold my hand? Will it be the same? And as Clapton wrote, "I must be strong ...and carry on."

Strong and carry on? There are many times when we wonder how we will find our way; we also wonder if we belong or are worthy to be in heaven, exactly like Clapton wrote in the song.

I never listen to this song without reminding myself that my hope to see Ben again in heaven is rooted in the words of Jesus.

Jesus' resurrection was a unique event. After Jesus rose from the dead, He told his followers, "Because I live, you will also live." (John 14:19)

On sad days, music brings me joy, but that joy pales in comparison to the hope and trust I have that one day in heaven there will be no more tears—only the tears a mysterious God collected in a bottle for reasons I do not know-- and that I shall see Ben once again; that he will know my name; that we will hold hands and that both of us will feel we belong.

"Will it be the same if I saw you in heaven?" Clapton asked. It will be *far* greater than we can imagine.

Nature

As a medical doctor dealing with children and teenagers now for almost four decades, I have been graced by good health all throughout my career. I have always aimed to live by example when it comes to cultivating wellness. I always set an intention to eat healthy, be active and to reduce stress.

Once again, little did I understand that my lifestyle habits were already being Divinely orchestrated to sustain me in a time of need—a time of bereavement.

At the time of this writing, I am 67 years young, and I am blessed to say that I am still a streaker. Not a naked streaker, but a runner who has maintained a daily streak of running now for the past 13 years—every day. I also managed to complete over one hundred marathons by the age of sixty.

Most of my training was done outdoors, surrounded by nature in mostly pristine environments. As a devout believer in the Source of nature, I truly feel that when I find myself training for marathons, not inside a gym, but outside in nature, God speaks to me via His creation. I read somewhere that before there was a written Bible—some call it "The Word of God"-- that nature served as the Word of God.

After the morning rituals of intimacy with my loving Source, the Highest Power for energy, inner peace, and enduring strength, and after learning from soul coaches and resting in mindfulness, attending consciously to what arises daily, I head to the door and lace up my Nikes— regardless of conditions outside my safe, cozy, peaceful home.

I have faced blizzards, incessantly pouring rain, slippery ice, air pollution, unusually warm temperatures, hail, sleet, and whatever Mother Nature dishes out in a rather Unmotherly manner.

Rockies

To be surrounded by tall mountains is one of the most soothing places to be. I am blessed to live close to Swiss Alps-like mountains. It is often there that my finite mind becomes aware of God's infinite love for me. Mindfulness which also can be defined as a form of remembrance, evokes feelings of peace; a sense of the Creator's infinite assurance; a place to take refuge from pain; a reminder of how these towering structures formed millions of years ago still represent, to this day, the grounding and steadiness I need to stand strong against storms.

Millions of visitors from all over the globe are consistently captivated by these mountains every year.

In *Wherever You Go There You Are*, Jon Kabat-Zinn has a chapter on mountain meditation. He explains:

> *"When it comes to meditation, mountains have a lot to teach, having archetypal significance in all cultures. Mountains are sacred places. People have always sought spiritual guidance and renewal in and among them. Mountains just sit. It remains still as the seasons flow into one another and as the weather changes moment by moment and day by day. Calmness abiding in all change. As we sit holding this image in our mind, we can embody the same wavering stillness and rootedness in the face of everything that changes in our lives over seconds, hours, and years."* (16)

Having to learn, day by day, to be mountain-strong after a major change, is not easy... and yet other parents have learned how to do that. So can I. With help from Above. With the help of mountains reminding me to be tall and strong.

***

I wish I had the skill to motivate all those who lost a loved one to find their own tools to cope. Tools to help at the inevitable lonely middle-of-the-night-moments. Tools that pass the test of time. Tools to move a suffering human from being mentally stuck to being free and unstuck. Tools that enable you to handle questions such as "How are you?", the way one mom in our grief group answers when others ask her how she is doing.

She always answers, "Terrible. But thanks for asking." That is one of *her* tools. I borrowed it for my own use.

In this chapter I merely wanted to talk about my own tools to handle adversity. These are the tools I have discovered which work for me. My prayers are that at least *one* of my daily habits may work for those who have to deal with major losses in their lives. Major losses leave us with a limp in that we never move forward like we used to be.

A scar is a scar.

There arrives a seminal moment when we arrive at a deep knowing that we will always limp; a knowing that all the days ahead will never be ideal. I am praying that the scars of life will indeed, like the Kintsugi example I gave in the preface, lead us to a customized way of remaining resilient.

The quest to move forward with resilience requires consistency. And to be able to do that, I want to talk about my dipstick moments in the next chapter.

The Dipstick Moments

In the old days, when technology was less sophisticated, car owners of cars with combustible engines made it a habit to regularly check the oil levels of their car's engines. The smell of engine oil still evokes memories of my dad pulling out a dipstick, wiping the oil off and re-inserting the dipstick to check the oil level.

This image captures my consistent habit of reviewing daily, weekly, and monthly my goals, my journals, the quotes I stored away for future books and, yes ...much to my wife and friends' chagrin...my best dad jokes—the ones who consistently make others laugh and say, "That was one of your better ones."

In the next chapter I want to share some of my consistent daily habits which I review often and on purpose—to the point where they have now become second nature.

22

Weekly Reviews

The greatest glory in living lies not in never failing, but in rising every time we fail.
—Benjamin Franklin

If life were predictable it would cease to be life and be without flavor.
—Benjamin Franklin

One of the founding fathers of the United States of America continues to teach through his timeless words. In addition to his pioneering work, and being an author, Benjamin Franklin was also known for his work as a scientist, inventor, diplomat, printer, publisher, and philosopher.

We are told that he cultivated a habit of reviewing his many goals regularly. He had thirteen qualities he always wanted to work on, so he decided to take the 52 weeks of every year, take his thirteen goals and cycle through them four times per year.

The thirteen qualities Franklin worked on were: gratitude, positive speech, tranquility, righteousness, gentleness, respect for others, physical health, productivity, resolution, order, frugality, truthfulness, and humility.

Two other men—one a Rabbi and another a leadership coach –inspired me to make weekly or monthly reviews my regular habit.

Rabbi Mordecai Finley calls his own daily habits "The Basic Wall of Virtue Practice." It is trademarked and can be Googled of course for those who want more detail. In some ways it overlaps with the Dale Carnegie principles of not criticizing, condemning, or complaining.

Leadership expert, Dr. Randal Stutman, claims that he is seen as wise, funny, and insightful, but that is mainly true, *not* because he is such a star, but rather because over decades he habitually reviews stories he enjoyed hearing, jokes he read and quotes he encountered. He is correct in saying that at first it may feel strange and contrived, but after practicing these habits they become second nature.

Before Ben died I made it a habit to regularly reviews my progress in three areas—my spiritual habits, my mental attitudes, and my physical health. Looking back, it was as if Destiny prepared me to be ready for this unexpected tragedy.

Over the past three years, the levels of these reviews have become deeper and more personal and meaningful as I continue to struggle and search for methods which sustain me the most during the grief journey.

Desiderata

A poem, *Desiderata,* written in 1927, starts with, "Go placidly amid the noise and haste, and remember what peace there may be in silence." It is worth reading the poem over and over and thus *remember* this precious poem's timeless wisdom. I read this poem at least once a week.

I have paraphrased the poem to fit my needs as a parent who lost a child.

Once again, as I write "a parent who lost a child," I am reminded that there is no single word for a human placed in this position—it is so uncommon and surreal. Our culture may have a term for a more common experience such as the death of a spouse. After such an event we then use the word "widow" or "widower." To have a child die before a parent? No word exists for that.

The author of *Desiderata,* Max Ehrmann, had the skill to use just the right words to describe the path which leads to things we want or desire. The word "Desiderata" means things wanted and desired.

Though the poem is not divided into three sections, I elected to do so because I wanted to make it very practical for my own use. I see our existence through three lenses: how I relate to myself, to others and, most importantly—above all—how I relate to God.

I am paraphrasing as I reflect on how the poem reminds me to:

- Speak the truth softly and clearly.
- Be authentic in that process.
- Avoid getting jaded and cynical.
- Avoid comparing myself to others.
- Enjoy making new plans.
- Stay interested in my calling as a doctor, writer, and athlete.
- Be humble.
- Strive to be happy.
- Be cheerful.
- Be gentle with myself.
- Be graceful in surrendering my youth as I transition into my senior years.
- Avoid the proliferation of fears and imaginations.
- Not be surprised at sudden misfortune.

Relating to others, the poem reminds me to:

- Be on good terms with others as much as possible.
- Listen to others and respect all people for all of us have important stories to share.
- Pay attention to tricksters and sham artists simply as a way to be wise rather than coming from a place of paranoia or cynicism.
- Avoid loud and aggressive people for, as the poems says, "They are vexations to the spirit."

Contemplating God, the poem reminds me every time I review it that I am a child of God, made in His image and that I have a right to be here as long as He allows it. Other reminders in relating to God as described in the poem are:

- Trust Him even when it is unclear why things happen the way they happen.
- Be strengthened by Him.
- Be at peace with Him.
- Accept that there are many versions of God, but all are ultimately rooted in love.

In addition to the poem, I also review—at least once a month—one of the least popular books in Scriptures found in the Old Testament. Some say this book is too dark and too morbid.

Ecclesiastes

This book depresses many in that it seems to say at the very beginning that life "stinks" and nothing is worth living for; all is in vain; you live and die and that even if you were a good person, you will face the same destiny as a "bad" person. What a negative way to start a book!

Before Ben died I rarely read Ecclesiastes for the same reasons most people avoid reading it. I found it too depressing and dark.

Today I count it as one of my most favorite books to read—not because of a morbidity that struck me after losing a child, but rather as a reminder of the fact that we must cultivate good priorities and never forget to enjoy life while we have it.

These are only *some* of the Ecclesiastes-based truths which gave birth to the ways I have decided to look at spirituality:

- God created people to be virtuous, but all make mistakes and follow our own ways. But at the very onset God planted eternity in the human heart.
- History repeats itself very often.
- Wisdom lights up a person's face and creates an aura of peace and calm.
- The greater the wisdom the more we think and thus tend to suffer.
- To everything there is a season.
- Sharpen the axe regularly.
- We rarely are able to see the whole scope of all things.
- No one can discover all God is doing under the sun; not even the wisest can do that.
- Nothing in life is certain. Sudden tragedy is part of life. Death is certain for all of us; not a single human being can prevent his or her own death.
- God has made everything, and it is there for us to enjoy; so, *enjoy* tasty food, good wine, *enjoy* wearing your favorite clothes and *enjoy* the presence of one's spouse.

- If you wait for perfect weather, you will never plant.
- We shall all have to give an account of all we did one day.
- Writing books are endless and too much study can wear us out.

Ecclesiastes ends with this reminder:

Have respect for the Creator and obey His wisdom.

Some translations of Ecclesiastes encourage us to *fear* God. These translations go on to claim that where fear exists, love is absent. This appears to be a major contradiction. How can we be commanded to love and then to be told to fear at the same time?

To use the word "fear" appears unwise. At the very least the word "fear" requires explanations because it may easily mean what it was not intended to mean. I suspect that by using the word "fear" it means to "Be in awe or wonder and thus obey out of love."

Carnegie

I will forever be grateful for the Carnegie Principles I learned when I took the training as a resident student in pediatrics in 1987. I also had the honour and opportunity to teach these principles as a Carnegie instructor between 1988 and 1999. The training is often seen as a class for those who dread public speaking, but it also teaches us how to relate to people and how to worry —ideally not at all, or at least less and less!

To this day these Principles are engrained in my psyche, and even so, I make it a habit to review them at least weekly.

Any person who lives by these principles will not criticize, condemn or complain; they will give honest and sincere appreciation; they will arouse in another person an eager want; they will become genuinely interested in other people; they will smile often; they will remember another person's name; they will be great listeners and encourage others to talk about themselves; they will talk in terms of the other person's interest. And they will make others feel important and do it sincerely.

It may be so easy to talk about my own problems and feel sorry for myself, but as Dale Carnegie so wisely suggested, talk about others *first* and do it from a place of sincerity. The fact is that if all humans were required to carry a sign around their necks which describes their own suffering in order that we may know and be forewarned, then nobody would be sign-free. We all need to be heard and seen. Just because I lost a child, I have no license to be unaware of the suffering of others.

Twelve Symptoms

On my list of things to review regularly—things which thus far has helped me navigate the grief path by Grace—is a list often encountered in the New Age community. Similar to Ben Franklin, I may take a week and focus *only* on one of the items on the list below, and by doing so, become more intentional and aware of my progress, or lack of progress.

The list is known as *The Twelve Symptoms of Spiritual Awakening*, and they are:

1. An increased tendency to let things happen, rather than make them happen.
2. Frequent attacks of smiling.
3. Feelings of being connected to others and nature.
4. Frequent overwhelming episodes of appreciation.
5. A tendency to think and act spontaneously rather than from fears based on past experience.
6. An unmistakable ability to enjoy each moment.
7. A loss of ability to worry.
8. A loss of interest in conflict.
9. A loss of interpreting the actions of others.
10. A loss of interest in judging others.
11. A loss of interest in judging self.
12. Gaining the ability to love without expecting anything.

Serenity

It is hard to be serene after the loss of a child or a loved one or anyone who meant so much to us. As we reflect on how to continue now that they are gone from this planet, we discover how elusive this serenity can be.

I have to constantly remind myself that as much as I would like to still have Ben with me... it is impossible. Of course, I want things to be different and normal—exactly as they used to be before he lost his battles. But it is so...and cannot be otherwise.

As I endeavor to move forward without Ben, I find there are reminders along the way. One such reminder, The Serenity Prayer, was written in 1926 for me to use almost one hundred years later. The prayer has become one of the most famous prayers ever written.

This prayer, written in 1926 by Reinhold Neibuhr, is a prayer well-known in the Alcoholics Anonymous community. The prayer is worth memorizing because there is absolutely no situation in this life where one cannot apply the wisdom contained in the opening lines:

> *God, grant me the serenity to accept the things I cannot change, the courage to change the things I can and the wisdom to know the difference.*

Other Habits Reviewed Daily

Before I get out of bed I quietly reflect on key affirmations. Most days I make it a habit to find things to be grateful for and I use these in my list of affirmations. I prioritize Spiritual affirmations which I intentionally speak out daily—such as "The Lord is my Shepherd" based on the psalm used at Ben's memorial service.

I have also found it most useful to journal down all the many blessings bestowed on me. I enjoy counting them one by one—always mindfully. There is ample scientific evidence regarding the benefits of journaling and gratitude.

Finally, I take the time to review a list of birthdays and anniversaries of family and friends, because I now know that these days are incredibly special. It really is a miracle to be able to celebrate these mile markers with others on the road called life.

I may not be able to take Ben out for dinner or a movie on his birthday or send him a card, but the least I can do is tell my friends and family how glad I am they are alive.

***

We can set daily or weekly intentions and aspire to embody more virtuous habits. Our paths may start off with good intentions, but we are all familiar with how we can so easily get distracted. I plead guilty to falling short when it comes to applying all the lessons I received from the Desiderata poem, reading Ecclesiastes, and memorizing the Carnegie principles.

But as we read at the start of the chapter, thankfully, Benjamin Franklin told us to remember that "The greatest glory in living lies not in never failing, but in rising every time we fail."

Those who have made a career out of teaching the anatomy of well-being tell us that there are at least four pillars to well-being:

- Awareness
- Insight
- Connections
- Purpose

My own well-being embodies all four of the above pillars—all by Grace. In Part II I wanted to share how I became **aware** of what was needed for me to do the hard work of grieving so that my suffering became *conscious* suffering. I became aware of the customized tools that work for me; I gained **insights** as to how these tools may be applied daily; I was still **connected** to my community of fellow grievers, my dear second family and, by Grace, I have found my **purpose** in all of this.

In the final part of this book, I want to talk about how we have the option to accept or reject Help from a Higher Power to sustain us in our time of grief. We may not always have key people to sustain us after a tragic loss; we may not always have the energy to sustain ourselves after a misfortune.

But we are invited to either accept or reject Help from Above, and in Part III I will humbly share my own personal journey of what I have done with my invitation.

PART III

23

Sustained By God's Love

I am sustained by the love of God. Here is the answer to every problem that will confront you, today and tomorrow and throughout time. In this world, you believe you are sustained by everything but God.
—Lesson 50. A Course in Miracles.

If one believes in a Deity, then the role of God when we suffer will *forever* be open to wide interpretation. I suspect every person will end up with his or her own understanding of the absence or presence of a God during times of suffering.

Faith, religion, spirituality all are very personal –just like grief... we all approach these tough topics in a very diverse and personal manner. A dogmatic, fundamentalist non-dualistic approach always will divide; and, sadly, *offend* most of the times.

I assume that the word "God," as part of the title of this chapter, may evoke in some readers various emotions related to their own beliefs regarding the existence of a Higher Power. To some the word "God" gives rise to significant aversions.

Based upon their own traumas, childhoods and experiences with organized religion and spiritual institutions... who can blame *anyone* traumatized by religion, for not wanting to read the rest of this chapter because of the word "God?"

As I mentioned previously, some influential spiritual teachers, such as Eckhart Tolle, intentionally and unapologetically prefer to avoid the word "God" for the very reason that it may potentially evoke aversions. Open any New Age book and one will immediately notice that the word "God" gets replaced by words such as: "The Divine," "The Universe," "A Higher Power," "Spirit," "Universal Intelligence," or "She." Sometimes a New Age teacher may also add "Whatever works for you" as a sincere way to not offend, but to be inclusive and non-judgmental.

My Intention

In writing this chapter I want to make sure readers do not see my views as preaching or imposing my interpretations on others. My views have been shaped by my experiences along the grief journey. They are my views and when I share them I do so with humility and sincerity.

If readers have very different views, I will respect those. My intention is simply to share my own views regarding the absence or presence of a Higher Power, God, at the time of deep suffering.

Thus far I wrote about my own experiences during the aftermath of losing a teenaged son to suicide—how various people sustained me and how I designed a customized plan to sustain myself.

My intention is to share, authentically how I am sustained by Love and how I, in turn, aim to make Divine peace my only goal, my purpose and my function.

***

Theologians, philosophers, mystics, poets, atheists, agnostics have written volumes on the topic of suffering. Words have the potential to be helpful in that they may explain to us the problem and the solution to our sufferings.

But as ancient Mystics wrote, there are times that when we are thirsty, the word "water" can be written ten thousand times in the sands of the desert, but what we need is a glass of water. We need *practical* help, not theological *theories* in times of sudden misfortune. In the acuteness of pain, being philosophical is not that helpful.

And as Rumi wrote: "From words alone you cannot know fire."

This chapter is simply a story—my story-- about the *experienced* transformational power of grasping there is strong possibility *also* of a Higher Power whose infinite love sustains us.

I cannot claim enlightenment as a spiritual seeker. But I do claim a new awareness—an awakening of sorts. Knowing that a spiritual journey always evolves, this is where I find myself at this time:

- Suffering can be experienced either *with* the help of God or *without* the help of God. Our free will leaves us free to decide for ourselves which fork to take when the road forks.

A Pastor With Experience

Pastor Rick Warren, author of the bestselling book, *The Purpose Driven Life,* also lost a son to suicide. Rick took six months off after his son Matthew died. When he returned as a pastor and spiritual coach, he taught a series on how to get through what you are going through. Rick explained that when a tragedy befalls us we have three options: we can allow it to define us, destroy us or develop us.

He went on to discuss how he surrendered to what happened by uttering these words:

> *"I am mourning but I am going to start moving.*
> *I am grieving but I am going to start growing.*
> *I am hurting but I am going to start healing.*
> *I am wounded but I am going to start walking.*
> *I am sad but I am going to step out."*
>
> *(Sourced from a Podcast by Warren with the title "How To Get Through What You are Going Through)*

By Grace, my family's tragedy has allowed me to look at suffering in a new light. But a faith-based approach to suffering is *not* for all people. They may find other avenues to cultivate resilience. Perhaps psychology or philosophy may be their anchors during storms.

Buddhist philosophies teach much about suffering.

The Buddha Who Knew his Purpose

Many who overcame their suffering claim that it was accomplished via Buddhism and without the help of a deity. The foundation of Buddhism rests firmly on the words of Siddhartha Gautama, the founder of Buddhism. Siddhartha was born 623 years before Christ Jesus was born. As far as we know Siddhartha never used the word "God."

The Buddha experienced and observed suffering which led him to contemplate the role of the mind and how mindfulness may alleviate suffering.

The Buddha was clear about his purpose when he said that the sole reason for his birth was to bring an end to suffering or, to paraphrase, he said that his only purpose was to teach the world how to manage life's inevitable sufferings by following the Four Noble Truths which contain the Eightfold Path.

Because the Buddha did not mention God or a Higher Power, many Buddhists do not believe in any kind of deity or god. They do believe deeply in being kind and compassionate and as the Dalai Lama once wrote, "Whether one believes in religion or not, there isn't anyone who doesn't appreciate kindness and compassion." He went on to add that his religion is kindness.

Buddhism is not a religion I subscribe to. But the fact that mindfulness, if done according to the Eightfold Path, resonated deeply for me along every inch of the path called "Accepting the death of a child."

Others Wrote About the Name That Cannot be Named

The Tao Te Ching, a classic Chinese text written around 400 BC, and traditionally credited to the sage Laozi, remains a great resource to those who suffer.

In the Tao Te Ching, we read that which can be spoken of, is *not* the enduring and unchanging Tao; that the name that can be named is *not* the enduring and unchanging name. We are told that having no name, the Tao is the Originator of heaven and earth; it is the Mother of all things.

According to the Tao's teachings that there *may well be* an Originator of heaven and earth and that there may well be a Mother of all things.

Ben had a mother, my dear wife Corinne, and he had a father; we both loved him very much. And based upon my own experiences since Ben died, I just do not have the faith to believe that there does not exist a Source who is an Originator and a Mother of all things.

As Ben's father I declare at the start of this chapter my position which may or may not land for some readers: I am sustained by the love of God. My story is that there is for me a loving God whose sustaining power sustains me in ways I *never knew before* my child decided to die by suicide.

I have *frequently experienced* the infinite love of an infinitely loving Being. I admit this Being is at times also a Big Mystery—unfathomable. Ineffable. Based upon personal experience, I totally agree with the words penned by Saint Paul when he wrote:

> *Oh, the depth of the riches both of the wisdom and knowledge of God! How unsearchable are His judgments and unfathomable His ways! For who has known the mind of the Lord, or who became His counsellor? Or who has first given to Him that it might be paid back to him again? For from Him and through Him and to Him are all things. To Him be the glory forever. (Romans 11:33-36)*

Personal Experience Alone

I wrote this chapter from my heart at a time when it is still recovering from being pierced. I am motivated by my experience of being sustained by the love of a mysterious Creator. My trust in this Infinitely wise and loving Power is solidly based on my life's experiences before, during and after the pivotal moment of dealing with the loss of a child.

The love between a parent and a child runs deep—perhaps deep enough that when a child dies, there really are not ideal words to describe the nature of this type of suffering.

In Part III of this book, I simply want to reflect upon the possibility of a Higher Power helping those who suffer greatly.

When Ben decided to leave this planet, his sudden and unexpected departure left a void. But he also left me with three options. I had to choose which of these three options would serve me the best:

- The tragedy could define me.
- The tragedy could destroy me.
- The tragedy could develop me.

This part of the book is a very personalized overview of what God meant to me and *continues* to mean to me on my own dark night of the soul.

It is not my purpose to proselytize, denounce, judge, preach or convince. I am not motivated to recruit others to my own understanding of who God is and what He is up to when we suffer unspeakable losses. That is not my aim. My aim is to extend kindness and love and make readers think for themselves regarding the deeper questions about a personal decision to consent to receiving Help from a Loving Source of *all*.

Some Key Questions

Senseless losses raise more questions than answers. I doubt if there is a bigger test than the test of dealing with a senseless loss. One constantly battles the pain of being *forever* plunged into darkness after such a loss.

The words uttered by Christ, "fear not for I am with you always," are deeply reassuring to me during this ordeal which I do not always understand.

The "I am with you always" part sustains me moment-by-moment-by-moment and is present like the air that I inhale— even in my sleep; like the pulse which began to beat while I was still in my mother's womb, and which will continue to beat, by Grace, until it is time to end this incarnation.

In this section, I will raise some tough questions which requires honesty and courage.

It would have been easy to ignore them. Because spirituality is so personal and possibly divisive I almost deleted this chapter a few months after I wrote it and after I was told "Your writing is very preachy."

These questions arrived like recurrent waves along the sandy shores of a vast ocean after Ben died. These are very deep and tough questions to contemplate. These waves of pondering the reasons for my lot in life bowled me over at times. But I always got up and faced them with Divine help.

Part III requires an open mind and I anticipate it may be seen as "too heavy" by some readers. That is fine. We all choose what works for us as the Buddha taught. My invitation is simple: read this section with an open mind and *see for yourself.* Only via your own personal experience do you decide how alleviating suffering will manifest.

If at the end of this section there is a sense that my words did not land, then remember the saying which was mentioned previously: "If the train does not stop at your station, it was not your train."

Reflecting deeply upon my faith journey during times of suffering, I came up with this list of questions:

- Where was God when our child died?
- Why did God not answer prayers?
- Why did God allow it to happen?
- What did I get in return for my faithfulness and for cultivating a spiritual practice prior to my loss? Did my loyalty waste time and energy?
- Is this Karma or payback for my past mistakes?
- What does it mean to trust?
- Can I ever regain the trust I had in the Divine?

***

I. WHERE WAS GOD WHEN OUR CHILD DIED?

For an atheist this is an easy question to answer: there is no God.

Perhaps an atheist will say it is *just something that happened. It happened maybe because of one thing leading to another. Overall, nobody runs the show after all. It is all random. Asking such a silly question is a total waste of time.*

The atheist, out of a deep sense of compassion when he hears a God-following believer talk about God, may feel sorry for the one who suffers. Perhaps the topic will be changed to something lighter out of fear that it may end a friendship. After all, we are encouraged to steer away from talking about sex, politics, and religion. It is too divisive and personal.

The mystical thinker —and I include myself in this category— acknowledges the possibility of a Higher Power. The mystical believer, convinced there is a living and loving God, also wisely makes room for the reality that God may be unpredictable, and as Paul wrote, "unfathomable."

Most mystics—the Christian mystic or Sufi mystic, or Jewish mystic — admit God does not always make sense.

An Evangelical Christian, *always* predominantly focused on the sinful nature of humans and the need for a Savior, will say "God was in the same place He was when his son Jesus died on the cross: on the throne in heaven, reigning over the cosmos and our planet."

The former believer—the one who lost faith as a result of being afflicted by misfortune—may have experienced a strong faith. The faith roots may have extended deep. Yet, the affliction choked the seeds which could have produced growth, embodied as wisdom gained from suffering. The cares of the world and other distractions caused the seeds to die.

Jesus taught in parables which were not always understood by his audience. Often, we read after a parable how Jesus had to explain his parables—*even* to his disciples. In Mark 4 there is a parable of exactly what I mentioned: seeds being choked by afflictions (Mark 4:17) Many former believers have told me they cannot believe in a God who allows suffering and apparently does very little to prevent it.

This former believer may say that he or she once believed in God and frankly have no energy or desire to even ponder this question of "Where was God when my child died?" To them any tragedy is a sign that God let them down in a time of need. They are sad, angry, deeply disappointed—and with good reason. Their seed of faith died or got choked by pain.

Many Views

When a parent loses a child to suicide, cancer, murder, or accidents we do not know exactly why this unfolded the way it did. The answer may be that God was in the same place He always was everywhere as an omnipresent, loving Energy. We simply will never know *for sure* until later.

My own belief is that when Ben died, God was omnipresent.

God, who referred to Himself as I AM when He spoke to Moses, the Hebrew leader whom God choose to lead the Jewish people out of captivity from Egypt, was *the same I AM* present when Ben died.

I AM was present then... and is present now... and forever more, because He is I AM.

This I AM, in allowing us to exist, also allowed us to exercise our free will.

Even in His presence, we are free to exercise a God-given free will. I will say this over and over in the pages to follow: free means free. At that moment when humans exercise their free will, God allows it —rather than control or change things.

Am I to be the One Who Blames God?

As a follower of the words, examples and teachings of Jesus, the Christ, I certainly am not blaming God for doing nothing to prevent Ben's death and allowing suffering to unfold. I do not blame Ben. I do not blame anyone or anything. Ben was brave. He lasted long...until he had enough of his own suffering and elected to leave.

A tight shoe was removed by a Child of God.

Ben was made in God's image, but when there was no more hope of a better future, he resorted to exercising his free will. Depression, resistant to therapy, killed Ben. Ben being allowed to exercise his free will, is one way to explain where God stood when Ben ended his own life. It was not God's will or fault.

It was the result of free will. And why free will exists and thus cause so much suffering remains a mystery.

I am sure there are those who will vehemently disagree because they believe God is *always* in *full* control. But one cannot have it both ways. Free means free.

Free Means Free

God is not a puppeteer who pulls strings and make us dance below. Free will, by definition implies that *even* the great I AM who decided to allow us free will, also decides to not interfere.

Free will *absolutely has* to be free—free from God playing a role at the time of free will being executed. Free from God's "interference." One can argue that we are in control—not God—when we execute our God-given free will. I have been told it is blasphemous to say God is not *always* in control. But think about it...

Logically if He is always in control, then he *must* control our will. But He does not control our free will; He wants it to be free for reasons that make little sense. (As a sidenote I have never received a satisfactory answer from Evangelicals who try to explain why God made Adam and Eve when He knew in advance, they will exercise free will and cause what they call "The fallen nature of man" or "original sin.")

He may change our hearts, but he is not allowed to change our will because He himself, Sovereignly, gave us free will. Free means free. Unless one considers the major role of free will plays in causing suffering, it can become very painful to those who trusted God to not let them down and to those who want God to always answer prayers. Free means free. Free from God... *Who does not over-ride what He decided to give us.* Why God allows free will, knowing that it can cause suffering, will forever remain a mystery to me.

This insight is so vitally important that I want to repeat it once more in bold letters and bulleted-- to underscore its total truth:

- ***Free means free, and thus free from God being in control when free choice is executed.***

What about other pivotal, communal, senseless sufferings since the beginning of the cosmos?

I have met a number of very passionate Jewish men and women when I attended synagogues to be present for weddings or Bar mitzvahs. So often when I asked them if they attend synagogue regularly, they answered, "I am Jewish but not religious."

When I respectfully show an interest in what they told me, I have noticed a pattern: Many of my dear Jewish friends tell me that they cannot believe in a God who allowed the Holocaust. How could a loving God allow Hitler, an evil man, to decimate millions of Jews?

My response usually is to simply listen to the reasoning of my friends who tell me they are Jewish but not religious. My views regarding free will may not be their views... so I do not go into why Hitler, an evil human being, was allowed to exercise his free will. My sincere Jewish friends have their reasons for rejecting God and who am I to judge?

Finally

So where was God when Ben died? He was ever-present and ever-loving; He remains unchanging and infinitely mysterious. His unchanging and infinite love sustains me now and forever. I *know* the love of God sustains me, deeply and in every cell of my being. I experienced it firsthand. To try and explain it with words may never work. Words fall short in this case.

***

II. WHY DID GOD NOT ANSWER MY PRAYERS?

I have been taught as a child, a young adult, and in my middle age that God *always* answers all prayers. Authors, ministers, and other teachers who teach this idea say that God's answers are "Yes," "No" or "Maybe later."

In the past I too believed that God answers *all* prayers.

After the death of my son, I do not believe that anymore.

After experiencing what Joseph Campbell refers to as the *Hero's Journey* or St. John of the Cross calls the *Dark night of the soul,* I have been transformed by the renewing of my mind. I have changed my mind. I *know* God does not answer all prayers.

However, I remain convinced that He answers most of our prayers, always in accordance with His own plans. I do not blame God for unanswered prayer, but to claim that He *always* answers prayers seem a bit too "tidy" and too contradictory. To say He always answers prayers works for those who had *all* their prayers answered *all* the time.

I used to buy into the notion that if I do my part, God is faithful to do His part, which is answer prayers as a result of my faith. That is easy to believe when all in one's life remains in order.

But then disorder struck as it did on January 1, 2020. Our prayers for Ben to stay alive even while being depressed were not answered.

Was it my own fault that my prayers for Ben to be kept alive were not answered? I doubt that very much. I do not blame anyone, and most importantly, I do not blame Ben. At the risk of being boringly repetitive, I remember that free will means *free* and thus *free from any other influence*

This misfortune did not change me from a believer into a doubter, but rather from an immature believer to a mature believer.

God is not a vending machine—where we do our part and God always give us what we desire or ask for. It is not simply a matter of us putting in the coins (do our religious works) and out comes God's favorable answers to all our prayers because He *owes* us His faithfulness.

Three-Part Evolution

When Ben died, I moved from a life of order to a life of disorder. The change was abrupt and immediate. I did not lose a pet, a car or a home, or a career or whatever material things.

I lost a child whom I deeply loved. It was an irreplaceable major loss and a sickening tragedy.

Not only did he die; he died by suicide, and he died in a violent way. The manner in which Ben died added many, many *extra* layers to my grief.

In his book *The Wisdom Pattern,* Franciscan monk and bestselling author Richard Rohr unpacks the three-part evolution many of us experience in our lifetimes. We move from order to disorder to reorder.

Those who have not yet suffered deep losses, but only success along the way, may find the book boring; those who suffered deeply, keep it close by and re-read it often. These sufferers have a deep knowing of the meaning of these three stages so well-articulated by Rohr.

It has taken three long years for me to slowly pivot in the direction of Rohr's notion of Re-order. I am not fully there yet, but I aspire to grow further and to be increasingly more aware of The Presence of God—even when my prayers that Ben be kept alive were NOT answered.

Sufficient Grace

Because my wife, perhaps more than me, continue to struggle with the question of how a loving God we trusted did not answer our prayers, I pondered the question of unanswered prayer and at just the right time I read the right words when I needed a deeper understanding:

"There was given me a thorn in the flesh to torment me. Concerning this I prayed to God three times that it might leave me. And He said to me "My grace is sufficient for you.

For power is perfected in weakness." (2 Corinthians 12:7-9)

Paul's prayer

Those who often read the Bible may be familiar with the story about the experiences of the man who wrote the majority of the New Testament. We learn what can happen when we pray for the end of suffering when we read about this famous Jewish scholar.

Saul of Tarsus, who later became Paul the Apostle after his conversion experience on the road to Damascus, wrote about how he as a devout and sophisticated, passionate Jew became a follower of Christ. He talks about a mystical experience he went through where he was taken up to a place he calls "The Third Heaven" We read that few others get to go to that place. Paul explained that it was Paradise and inexpressible words were heard. Because not all people get to experience this Third Heaven, Paul felt special. Full of wisdom and full of spiritual insights, downloaded from God above, via his pen into what Christians call the inspired Word of God, Paul became the victim of his ego-self.

As a result, Paul struggled with pride. A thorn of some kind was given to him and caused him much suffering. What the thorn actually was—real or metaphorical—we are not told. How exactly the thorn was given to Paul we are not told. Once again, some who always are ready to ignore mysteries, and come up with apologies for God, have all the answers. But they too speculate that perhaps it was Paul's own ego. And some claim that if Paul had more faith his prayers would have been answered.

We are told Paul prayed at least three times for the thorn to be gone. Was his prayer answered? No.

Not at all. The thorn was *never* removed. The thorn's aversion was to remain forever. But what really caught my eye are these words that landed in the center of my suffering heart: "My grace is sufficient" and "Power is perfected in weakness."

Paul prayed for his tormenting to stop, and his prayers were never answered. Grace was enough. Paul was weak, but also powerful as a result.

The story of Paul's thorn and unanswered prayer is frequently used in the context of unanswered prayer.

But what about Jesus himself? He too prayed to be spared the pain of crucifixion. His prayers were not answered. I doubt He blamed God. I doubt He lacked faith. And I doubt God tried to convince Pontius Pilate to *not* exercise his free will—which was to allow Christ Jesus to be crucified and suffer.

Divine Strength

Ask any grieving soul how they feel most days, and many will declare "I feel so weak; I am not sure I can go on. I wish this will end soon; I am so confused and fearful."

CS Lewis the author of *The Problem of Pain*, noted after his wife died, people who grieve are knocked down, but after they get up and try to walk again, they notice their gait is different. They limp. Never will they be without the limp caused by their perpetual pain. They may find it less painful as time passes, but the limp will linger until the last breath is taken.

Lewis explains in his pivotal book how the problem of pain can be managed with Divine Strength as the primary source of power.

The reality is that the scar caused after my heart got pieced will never be gone. It is indeed a thorn, not in the flesh, but in the soul—deeply embedded forever.

It is almost four years since Ben left, and I have experienced what I experienced; I know what I know; it is hard to explain and perhaps there is no need to explain this at all, for I know daily what is true for me: Grace is *more* than sufficient. Power from Above is perfected in weakness. Even when my limp will last forever.

Our hearts are aching years after Ben left. The pain is hard to put into words. It is ineffable to those who never buried a child. And yet I am sustained by the love of God.

***

III. WHY WAS BEN'S DEATH ALLOWED TO HAPPEN?

Many best-selling authors in the Christian community have written extensively about why God allows suffering and many have bravely attempted to make sense of things when God does not make sense. Some of these authors have lived lives of relentless victory and thus never had to face a dark night of the soul—at least not by burying a child.

As a result of meeting thousands of souls who came to them for counseling at a time of deep suffering, these authors have learned what they learned *indirectly.* They may not have had their faith tested by burying an innocent child. They exercised their gifts of articulating their thoughts on suffering via best-selling books. Their books have helped millions of readers. But they do not always write from a place of personal *experience.* Of course, there are exceptions.

After many hours of reading various books, contemplating my lot, aiming to not get derailed by doubt or discouragement, applying centering prayer as the pathway to contemplative prayer, I have no *sure* and final answer as to why God allowed Ben to die.

My point in writing about why God allows terrible things to happen to good people is that none of us can really be 100% sure our books or ideas are watertight and fool-proof.

I explained earlier, for now free will makes the most sense in my quest to comprehend why it happened. Some spiritual teachers explain that the soul consists of our will, mind, and emotions. And many Christian ministers believe that satan is the root of *absolutely all evil.*

satan

A number of Christians told me after Ben's death that he killed himself because satan got into him. Please note that in all my writings the word "satan" will never be capitalized—to me, when we capitalize a word, we do that to signal great credibility.

I read there was once an angel who decided to rebel against God and then became a fallen angel named satan. But I refuse to capitalize this word. My concern with the satan explanation is that too often satan is used as an excuse to "park" the unexplainable. It easily becomes a cop-out. Free will explains to me why my dear son decided to leave this planet. And God did nothing, because free will is free from God. God allowed it. But why He did that is a mystery for now.

I cannot say this often enough: I never will blame God for my suffering. When we get to the last chapter of this book —the topic of how it is possible to love God more after misfortune—I shall write, with authentic detail, about how the Divine mysteriously and gracefully guided me after sickening tragedies.

The Fear Magnet

Some Christians teach that when we fear we create our own suffering. Supposedly, we attract suffering. It is all our fault. In the classic book about suffering, the book of Job, we read at the beginning of the book how satan had to ask God for permission to test Job. Only after seeking permission does satan go to work and cause all kinds of trouble in Job's life. Again, I have noticed how some Bible teachers ignore that part of the story and then go on to blame poor Job for his own misfortune. Why?

Because he caused it himself by being filled with fear, which attracted Job's trouble according to these well-meaning teachers. If they want to teach about how unhealthy it is to fear that is one thing. But to blame an innocent man, Job? Some would say it is unfair to Job because God gave permission to stan to almost destroy all that belonged to Job.

But if sincere Christians disagree, it is their right, and we must agree to disagree and still love one another—more so in the midst of deep suffering.

Fear is indeed the opposite of love. But even Jesus feared his death because he understood what physical pain was awaiting him. The incarnate Christ was human; he was deeply troubled, just like me; just like us. I doubt Ben died because of my human proclivity to harbor fear —-even for a brief moment. I admit that at times I struggled to cast down imaginations and bring thoughts captive to obedience of the Gospels—the Good News. But I do not believe my fear caused my son to die.

Not so long ago someone explained that suffering in this live can be explained by our soul contracts. These are supposedly agreements we make with other souls before both souls are incarnated.

Soul Contracts

There are numerous reasons to explain why so many teens are depressed, but unlike Ben, the majority do not end their lives by suicide. My finite mind may be able to study, read books, contemplate, and pray often. But as much as we humans want certainty and agency, the reality of our limited understanding hits home when, despite our best efforts, we still fall short.

If we cannot fully grasp the causes of suffering... are there others, wiser than ourselves? Philosophers, best-selling authors, spiritual gurus, mindfulness teachers, preachers, and life coaches all may have ideas to account for reasons which lie at the roots of senseless losses. I have even heard some say that when a child dies, it is because we signed a soul contract with that child prior to his or her birth.

To explain a soul contract: Imagine Ben before his birth making an agreement with me and God that he will come to earth; that I, of all people, will be his dad; that he will be depressed and that his depression will cause his death at age sixteen. The point of the death? So that I, his dad who signed a soul contract with Ben, can make the world a better place by helping other teens not die from depression. I find it hard to buy into this kind of speculation.

Partial Seeing at Best and Not in Charge

I have enjoyed over the years to always approach anything with a beginner's mind. I read somewhere that those of us with a beginner's mind come to a point where we realize that in cultivating such a mindset, we soon learn that answers will remain elusive and mysterious. All our beginner's minds will find there is no end. We navigate beginnings that never end.

As a result of Ben's death, I have concluded that my vision can be 20/20 if I see the way Richard Rohr explains our vision when he wrote that most of us do not see things the way they are, but we see things as we are. He adds that "How we see is what we see." But even then, it is ultimately partial seeing.

As I mentioned earlier in this book, I also have discovered another way of seeing other than with 20/20 clarity. In Proverbs twenty, verse twenty-four, we see that a Higher Power directs our steps. We are not in control as much as we think we are. The verse ends with this reminder: "Why bother to figure out everything along the way?"

For many years after Ben's passing, I tried to figure things out along the way. I do not have the exact answer, but I have been led to look at Scriptures which I can either accept or reject. My aim in studying Scriptures is to see better; to gain insight.

In Psalm 115: 2 and 3 we see, "Why should the nations say, "Where now is their God?" But our God is in the heavens: *He does whatever He pleases.*"

The Great I AM does whatever He pleases. I agree with that. But I respectfully have to add to Scripture that even if it is true, He is not only in heaven, but He is also actually omni-present. He is everywhere and always busy doing what He wants to do, but in a benevolent way—especially so after humans exercised their free will in unloving ways and apart from His will.

When we read that God does whatever He desires, it does not mean that He does not love us. It does not mean that he forgets us. We may feel forgotten but as Meister Eckhart wrote, "God is at home. It is we who have gone for a walk."

It is not always possible to understand everything because God can go into hiding.

The God Who Hides.

There are many times when the most devout believers experience the fact that God hides himself.

In Isaiah 45:15 we read that He is a God who hides himself. In the same chapter, Isaiah 45, God states over and over—so as to drive the point home I suspect—that "I am the Lord. There is no one else. I am righteous and a Savior. There is none except me. There is no other. Words have gone forth from my mouth in righteousness and will not turn back. And all those who are angry at God will be put to shame." (Isaiah 45:18-24)

I doubt we will ever get to a place where all theologians and spiritual seekers will agree 100% on the causes of suffering. We can choose to get angry at God, but in the end our infinite minds will be put to shame. The topic is too nuanced to attractively package it and tie a ribbon on top of the box containing insights and wisdom.

The good news is that after sickening tragedies there is A Presence who may hide Himself in terms of explaining our questions, but My Infinite Lover has provided, by grace, a light in my heart.

This truth is the reason I have taken a pause here to wipe tears of joy from my eyes and to blow my nose. It is wonderful news that I, of all people, have been allowed to offer my heart as a venue for The Light. The Holy Spirit helps me become more and more aware of the Presence of a God who may at times appear to be absent—the God who for mysterious reasons loves to hide. But always chooses to love.

The mystic, St. John of the Cross, wrote in poetic terms when he said of his own dark night of the soul that on a dark path, he had no light to guide him except for the Light which burned brightly within his heart.

I have experienced the warmth of such a light many times in my grieving heart.

***

IV. FRUITS OF ENDURING

Some Christians believe that if they do their part then God—who is always faithful and honest—is obliged to do His part and protect us from harm. But is that true? Why did my faith not translate into having all my children still alive?

Ben grew up in a faith-based home. When he was still a young cute baby, Corinne and I made a promise, in public in front of an audience who were free to hold us accountable, that we will raise all our children in accordance with the teachings of Christ. What this means specifically, and succinctly, is that all in our family aspired to obey what Christ said we should do:

- Love God with all our hearts.
- Love with all of our soul.
- Love with all our minds.
- Love our neighbors.
- Love ourselves.

Notice that Christ did not say we must worship him. He said, "follow me." Notice to that Christ was not a Christian; Christ did not belong to a denomination or a church; He did not author a book. He did not seek power and control. He was not incongruent. He specifically said that His task was not to judge and condemn but to teach us about humility, patience, love, and compassion. And because of all of this, I felt comfortable to make a commitment and set an intention to teach all my children about the Christ consciousness.

I was confident that if I were to do my part, then Ben's Creator would do His part. I was in partnership with the Divine. I felt he had my back.

All through Ben's early years Corinne and I were told that we were good parents. I always refused to be like the rooster who takes credit for the sunrise. So, I *never* responded to others by saying, "Yes indeed we are good parents; we read parenting books; we lead by example; we are good Christians; and if you want to invite us to give talks on good parenting... feel free to ask us—we will be there to enlighten you with our insights"

As a spiritual being, a doctor, and a father I evolved as a parent and understood how complicated parenting actually can be. It is especially complicated if we are given the assignment to parent a child with depression, anxiety, giftedness and on top of that all an attention deficit challenge. Ben had *all four* of these challenges.

As I explained earlier, there was a season when we attended a church which taught that if we as believers do our part then God has no choice to respond to us and do His part to make us successful. A minister with millions of followers confidently made the point that, "God is obligated to respond to our efforts, because if He does not do that, He then becomes a liar. And God cannot lie."

Is it any wonder then that when some faithful believers subscribe to such teachings, and then get plunged into a tragedy, not of their own making, they will abandon their faith? They clearly struggle with this thought: *If I was faithful to God, why was God not faithful to me?*

Regardless of what happened to me and my family, I am able to endure *not* because I feel I can approach God as a vending machine; *not* because my finite mind makes it possible, but rather because an Infinite Mind, a Benevolent Mind has lent to me all that I have and all that I can become. I am merely looking after what I have been given by Grace. I thus am able to write these words from my heart. I see my stewardship as sacred.

To paraphrase the teaching of a Christian mystic from the 14th century, I am not saying "Look at what I have accomplished and look at how I endure", but instead I say, "Look at Who has made this possible."

By enduring I have tasted the fruits that come from a partnership with my Creator. This partnership is firmly based on these two affirmations I make almost daily in my quest to stay strong:

- "God, I do not understand why this has happened to me; something I never thought would happen in my wildest dreams."
- "But God, I trust you fully and unconditionally because I believe I am sustained by Your love in mysterious ways." I have set a specific intention to endure—regardless of my own understanding.

***

V. KARMA

The need of many humans to carry guilt and blame themselves for things that go wrong may lead to the question of, "Is this Karma or payback time for my past mistakes?"

If there is such a thing as karma and if it is true that at some point, we ultimately reap what we sow, then I like to think of karma not as punishment embodied in the task of burying an innocent child, but rather as being guided by a merciful and forgiving Creator. We offer our consent, and the consequences are karma—His love, forgiveness, and relationships with us.

But not all can accept forgiveness as the next story will show.

In his book Th*e Anatomy of Hope*, author Jerome Groopman, MD, writes a story about a woman who was diagnosed to have breast cancer. This patient became unusually restless when Dr. Groopman explained to her that she had a relatively good prognosis for survival.

Later it was revealed by the patient, shortly before she died, that she had an affair which her husband never knew about. The patient felt that her punishment was dished out by God in the form of cancer and that she deserved to die. She did not believe in a forgiving God as much as she believed in a God who is righteous, and true to His word; a God who says He loves us, but he also must punish us because He hates our sins. She had no hope because she felt she deserved the punishment of death.

I have observed that human nature always seems to look for explanations; we feel safe when there is certainty. No wonder then that when tragedy grips us and shakes us back and forth, like a dog shakes it prey, captured by it long, sharp fangs...that we seek answers and explanations. Many resort to using negative consequences (karma) as the reason for suffering.

So many times, these are the many questions that swirl in our minds, proliferating when we are in pain and alone:

- What have I done to deserve this?
- Is it payback time for all the moments when I intentionally or unintentionally caused others to suffer? Or perhaps it is not punishment but mere consequences—cause and effect?
- Could this be the result of my ancestors who were ruthlessly cruel to the underdogs and the outcasts of society?
- It has been said that what we sow we shall reap, and could this tragedy be the result of poor choices we made in our past?

You will Have Trouble

Ever since I decided at a teenager--ironically, the same age as Ben's age when he decided to leave—to follow Christ Jesus' examples in words and deeds, I have seeked a relationship with God, Christ, and the Spirit.

Looking back, I have absolutely no regrets. To sense the Presence of an unfailing God and to hunger and thirst for union with the Infinitely caring and wise Creator, is indescribable. The quality of my life has always been such that I experienced true and lasting inner peace. That has never changed. I know how it feels to be forgiven for my mistakes.

What changed after Ben died is that I now understand better the words of Jesus, so often conveniently ignored by those who teach when we do our part God is obliged to do His part.

These words are found in one of the Gospels where Jesus says very clearly that we, in this life, *will* have trouble. Nobody gets a free pass. It is a given. (John 16:33)

I recalibrated my heart to pivot away from a quid pro quo relationship to a more meaningful and mature connection where I now grasp that He mystically always remains close to me—regardless of my circumstances. And perhaps more so when I am in pain and anguish.

I remain grounded in that infinite lovingawareness; a Christ-consciousness, rooted in the knowledge that to be mindful is one thing; mindfulness is also about always remembering to remember; to always attend, recognize and be aware is what Zen teachers teach so well. But to take it to the higher level for me is to seek a higher level of consciousness, not only at the mind level, but also at the deeper core or heart level.

With the Universal Christ as my mentor, I now know so much more about humility, compassion, love, and patience than I did before Ben decided to leave. As I continue to mystically experience the love of God sustaining me every moment of my life, I have a deeper level of trust than ever before. I am mindful that I have a Source.

What Happened to Trust?

Once again as we look back over the previous pages, I want to *humbly* acknowledge that my understanding is only partial. To ask, "Where was God when my child died?" or "Why did God not answer prayers?" and "Why did a loving God allowed this to happen" are very natural in terms of the way our psyche functions. To ignore our innate wiring to seek answers to our suffering and to be so spiritual that we tell those who ask questions and simply trust is called spiritual bypassing.

Bypassing happens when our quest to be spiritual ignores our psyche and its desire to get to a stage of radical acceptance.

The same curious psyche, who can choose to never trust God to sustain us by his Love, can pivot to a deep anger. In our anger we may wonder, *"God I served and followed You and this is what I got in return? Could it be that I wasted my time and energy? How then can I move forward and trust you God.?"*

Why have I so far not answered the last two questions on the list enumerated at the start of this chapter? (What does it mean to trust and can lost trust ever be regained?)

I have decided that these two questions—very important and perhaps the most important on the list of questions— must be dealt with intentionally in the next chapter, because to me that is what being sustained by the love of God ultimately means.

24

Trust

Happy is he who trusts in God.
—Proverbs 16:20

Almost six weeks after Ben's passing into another realm, I found myself running along the coastline in La Jolla, California, one morning. It was as if I was running in Paradise.

The conditions were perfect in that the Pacific Ocean was calm, its smooth surface dotted with swimmers in black swimsuits, kayakers gliding back and forth, and the occasional seal announcing its presence with a joyful bark. Fragrant flowers populated the landscape around me, and the sweet sounds of chirping of birds echoed through the crisp morning air. The soft green grass was covered in sparkling dew. My eyes were caught by the sunrise, coloring the distant mountains bright orange and then slooooowly transitioning it into a bright yellow color as dawn unfolded in silent splendor.

At that moment I became overwhelmed by a profound sense of despair, confusion, and loss. I was missing Ben so much and wished he were there right next to me to also enjoy the natural beauty which evoked such awe and wonder. I sobbed and fell to my knees. I lost any sense of time.

Then suddenly, in the spirit realm, I heard these gentle words:

> *"Ben is safe with me, and you need not worry about him. He loves you and is not suffering anymore. What you are seeing*

> *now does not even come close to what you and Ben will see together one day. I am your shepherd and will guide you in the days ahead."*

It was indeed a profoundly impactful moment—one that was unique and healing. The image I had of where we found Ben's body that fateful night is now replaced by the image of this mystical moment at sunrise next to the ocean in La Jolla. It was there that I received a healing gift from heaven.

Whom to Trust?

I have noticed that when people suffer, they become seekers automatically.

They seek relief. All humans who suffer seek some form of an anchor—something which stabilizes them in the midst of storms. The unpleasantness of pain hinders all of us; we want relief; we look for solutions. We yearn for an escape. We wish we could find the trust that somehow this nightmare will end. And if it never ends, if we never get to a place of acceptance, then at least we want to be able to trust that we will find a customized path to move forward.

The hindrances of doubt and fear and uncertainty overwhelm us when we are not on guard. We feel weak; we feel lost; at times we feel so lonely that we convince ourselves that there is *nobody* out there who can help us; *nobody* understands our pain.

Grief is one of the loneliest journeys any human being can be forced to endure. No wonder we seek; we seek out of a deep desperation to understand the "why?", and we are afraid when there are no answers.

As a form of self-preservation, this part of human nature, the need to discover an anchor called trust, is an automatic response—similar to our arms that automatically shoot forward to protect ourselves when we fall forward. We desire that there be order. We look for what makes the most sense.

Regardless

In trying to deal with emotional pain, the question inevitably becomes quite simple: where are the best places to seek solutions? Who can I trust? Is there such a thing as North Star which in dark times becomes my hope and my guide? How did others get through their own dark nights of the soul?

Some will return to work the very next day after losing a loved one. Work is their purpose and calling. It brings meaning. It becomes one of the few stabilities at a time of misfortune and confusion. It may be an escape, but it may also be a way of service.

As the Dalai Lama once observed, when we give, we give for selfish reasons; we give to receive. One writer reminds us that the fragrance of a rose clings to the hand who gave it away. And other writers have taught that giving and receiving are the same. By serving others we find meaning. It makes us feel better when we encounter the helpers high. At least at work there is a temporary escape, and we feel needed. This gives us a sense of meaning—a reprieve from mental trauma, where unlike a physical cut, there are no stiches to at least bring the wound together for now.

Some will resort to exercise. That too is a way to escape and numb the pain. As Tony Robbins once said, "Motion creates emotion." Increase the blood flow to the brain and we think with clarity; our consciousness becomes elevated. As my coach will claim, "We "uplevel" ourselves to a higher vibrational energy."

Energy flows unhindered. Oxytocin, the feel-good hormone, floods and soaks our being. But h relief—good as it may be—is only transient.

Nature, especially to those who grieve, provides stability and hope. It becomes their towering, stained glass cathedral where they are surrounded by stable mountains—structures which existed millions of years before we arrived and structures which will still tower above many generations yet to be born. The symbolism of seemingly ageless mountains evokes thoughts of standing strong and towering above. And this goes on and on and on for as long as Nature allows it to be so.

Or we observe waves coming and going... standing on the shores of oceans which stretch far away into distant unknown horizons. We smell the ocean air; we hear seagulls communicate in "seagullese" in the clear blue skies above the pounding waves.

There are times when I experience the sacred majesty of nature in such depth that it makes me emotional. I pause, observe, being fully present in the nowness of it all... and cry.

I have been told by some friends that they would rather experience God in nature than in any church. Even friends who do not believe in a Deity seek solace in nature, because they *know* it makes them feel good. Their escape is to meditate on the *creation* rather than the *creator* whom they decided does not exist. Could it be that the Creator, anonymously, is the One who does the stirring of their hearts when they experience a knowing in nature; an experiential knowing that it is there where they find their trust on the path to peace?

Overwhelmed, by creation and the peace it brings... we just sit, fully present, absorbing the unspeakable tranquility these mountains provide. A walk next to the ocean may remind us of the always-shifting tides. Waves come and go. Tides go out far from the shoreline, and we wonder jokingly if someone forgot to put a plug in the drain. We walk out on the sand which in hours will be covered with waves again. The contact of our feet with sand, water and grass evokes thoughts of being grounded. But this too does not last. Such is life: ups and downs. Things arise and then pass. Clouds come and go. Nothing stays the same.

Sadly, some of us are impatient and want *immediate* relief. We use drugs or alcohol to mop up the blood left after the beast of trauma took a bite out of our being. We convince ourselves that we can stop anytime and that our solution which works well thus far will be needed *only* until we recover from this misfortune. It works for a while... until it ceases to provide lasting relief.

At that point, not feeling heard, seen, or understood, and failing to find our customized anchor, having lost all hope, some decide to leave this planet. Some leave a note; others just leave without any clues to help those who remain. Family members of the one who decided to leave remain clueless.

Preparation

My personal faith journey started in my teen years in a place called Durban, where I grew up in this port city, located on the eastern coast of Southern Africa. In 1972, at the age of sixteen, I experienced a spiritual awakening and made the choice to trust Christ to be my mentor and role model. I never regretted this moment.

Over the next fifty years I personally experienced the meaning of bathing in unconditional love and forgiveness. Numerous times I have experienced that my heart was made in such a way only God will do. It humbles me as I look back and see how every chapter in my life, Providentially, prepared me for the worst day of my life.

In the years following 1972, I experienced a sustaining faith. I define my own faith journey as the experience of a confident knowing that there is a Higher Power --even when that Power does not always make sense. My certitude may have waned at times, but it never ran dry.

I have chosen to think of faith in terms of two words: *unconditional* trust. It always was an anchor for me since the age of sixteen; it rooted me into deep, fertile soil; when other storms arrived unexpectedly –like gusts of winds assaulting tall trees—I managed... by Grace... to stand strong. Despite the teachings of some pastors and ministers, having faith does not exempt anyone from catastrophes, and my moment of testing arrived just after midnight on December 31, 2019. It suddenly became my biggest test ever.

The day after my child succumbed to suicide was the day when I saw with absolute clarity that all the days prior to that fateful day were days of synchronistic preparation.

Every time I read scriptures, paid attention to meaningful sermons, read books, listened to podcasts, spent time in contemplative prayer, journaled, memorized key verses...these activities— without me realizing that—were moments when seeds were planted. I thought I was merely cultivating a personalized spiritual practice. Little did I know at the time that those seeds would bear much fruit—fruit which sustained me when I needed it the most.

Religion

This chapter deals with trust and specifically discovering which anchor allows us best to cultivate trust. Faith helps me to unconditionally trust.

Too often faith is confused with religion, and by organized religion many think of dogma, theology, tradition, denominations, and the all too common prideful us-versus-them mentality.

At the time of this writing, I cannot recall times in our recent culture where aversions toward religion have been any stronger, where divisions have been wider and where an increasing number of people have looked elsewhere for their peace of mind. Many simply lost trust in God and religion.

By referring to "elsewhere" I have noticed teachings on the topic of a higher cosmic consciousness abound like never before. But what specifically is this particular consciousness about? Us? Others? A supreme Creator in charge of the cosmos?

I have many friends who told me that they are not into religion—any religion. I usually ask them to explain, but *only* if they are comfortable, why religion is such an aversion. So often I hear, "The church is full of hypocrites," or "Many wars were fought in the name of religion," or "Religion divides us, and I do not like the us-versus-them mentality of many zealous, dogmatic, fundamentalist Christians who proselytize." Many also add that churches have become too political and keen supporters of narcissistic politicians who lie relentlessly.

Some of my friends even refer to all Christians as being "Goody two shoes" or "Pollyannish." Sometimes I can see their point of view clearly.

If religion indeed leads to more division and if it often seems to be more about rituals, dogma, and tradition then the words of Richard Rohr, a Franciscan monk, invites us to consider alternative views. In his book *The Universal Christ,* Rohr puts it this way:

> *"After all, there is not a Hindu, Native, Buddhist, Jewish, Islamic or Christian way of loving. There is not a Methodist, Lutheran, or Orthodox way of running a soup kitchen. There is not a gay or straight way of being faithful, nor a Black or Caucasian way of hoping."*

Rohr goes on the make a point that religion is too often known for being *transactional* rather than for its original intent: to be *transformational.*

Having heard clearly from some of my best friends that religion offends them, I respect the fact that they have not yet found faith to be their anchor.

Practical and authentic religion—personal transformational faith-- has not yet been their experience they tell me.

Once again my intention is not to judge. I am not being preachy. I am simply saying that, by grace, I have experienced that *transformational spirituality* is an ineffable joy.

In the grief journey there is no right or wrong way to grieve. In this chapter I am merely sharing my own journey and how I will forever be grateful for my own experiences with an Infinite loving Mind, a God who is a very present help in times of trouble, a Christ consciousness which saves me from unnecessary suffering, and a wise Spirit who faithfully guides every step of my journey. I fully trust my Source—even when I have questions. I don't doubt. But I often ask and wonder. And my Creator stays patient with me being curious because perhaps it is a way to stay close as we "wrestle" with one another.

I have been transformed by my belief in the Universal Christ—not a denominational or Cultural Christ. By consenting to experience the presence of a deeper consciousness and awareness—a Christ consciousness--I remain sustained.

I know with absolute certitude that when I am weak, I am strong, and that Grace is more than sufficient. The power of Grace is made perfect in my weakness. I shall never understand why I have been allowed to experience a deep inner awareness of a loving, wise, and omnipresent Creator—let alone write about it. I shall forever be humbled by the power of Grace to provide *perfect* peace beyond understanding; peace that continually guards my heart and mind.

Key Scriptures for Contemplation

My habit has never been to ingest and digest Scripture like fast food. I prefer to be like the ancient Mystics who first read scriptures, reflected on what they read, responded to the discoveries made, and then relaxed peacefully in the end—free from thoughts, emotions, time and struggles with the self.

For as long as I am allowed to live, I shall never rush though Scriptures in one year to say, "I did it." If I were to do that it would be my ego at work, rather than the childlike true self, seeking a beginner's mind by staying teachable. To be still is to hear Spirit talk in a still small voice.

In my journal I keep records of scriptures which continue to speak to me at a heart level.

In Latin, "Lectio Divina" refers to the reading of scriptures and then *intentionally* and *unhurriedly* pausing after reading them. Paging through a recent journal, and enjoying the royal blue color of the ink which flowed effortlessly from my European-made fountain pen, I noted seven reasons why I have decided to continue trusting in a Higher Power, the God of my salvation:

- God created me. (Isaiah 43:7)
- God knows me by name. (Isaiah 43:1)
- God thinks about me. (Psalms 139:17)

- God defends me. (Exodus 14:14)
- God has plans for me. (Jeremiah 29:11)
- God is a refuge. (Psalm 62:8)
- God is always with me and will never forsake me. (Matthew 28:20)

As I look back over almost seven decades of being alive, I see how the vicissitudes of living a full and colorful live, has taught me that I may not have controlled as much as I thought.

In the past I went through a season where I was convinced by teachers espousing a Pollyanna faith system or New Age belief system that we *alone* determine outcomes. In these belief groups almost everything has some positive reframe or explanation.

I bought into those beliefs and for a season they served me well-- but after the death of a child, I have taken the off ramp from this freeway of "certainty." We do not control all of life; we do not just manifest with the magic wand of our mouths; we are not magnets which magically attract whatever we desire. The law of gravity *always* works; the law of attraction may work for some, but unlike gravity, it does not *always* work.

On my desk I keep a small dice as a visual reminder of the words in Proverbs 16:33 where we read:

"We may throw the dice, but God determines how they fall."

I have surrendered to the fact that aiming to explain all and understand all, ultimately is futile. I used to have an "addiction" to grasp the roots of all suffering. So often, in looking at the reasons for our incessant and pernicious needs to think and understand, we see how it relates to our nature to cling to our egos. Author and New Age spiritual teacher, Eckhart Tolle, says "We are addicted to thinking." He embodies and invertebrate belief in the power of the present *only*—without any thoughts, feelings, or emotions. Just be.

As I continue to navigate life without my son, I am motivated by the Serenity Prayer—I do not control everything. Although I am a part of God, I am not God who can do whatever He pleases.

To let go is to surrender *fully*... 100% and not 99.9999999%; to resist is a sure path to further suffering. Trusting in God, not for an explanation, but rather for His love to sustain me in the aftermath of suffering has been my salvation—if one defines salvation as being set free from suffering.

I will Exult

In the Bible, a man named Habakkuk talks about his lot of his world (Habakkuk 3:17-19) He goes on to say, "Thought the fig tree should not blossom, and there be no fruit on the vines; thought the yield of the olive should fail and the fields produce no food; though the flock should be cut off from the fold and there be no cattle in the stalls. Yet will I exult in the Lord, I will rejoice in the God of my salvation. The God of my strength who makes me walk on my high places."

Often when I walk past Ben's room I remember the writings of Habakkuk, and in my heart declares that though Ben's room may be empty: though Ben's life did not last as long as most people's lives; though we will never see him go to higher education or see him get married or see him hold his first child in his arms; though we will never know what his life could have been had he stayed alive...Yet will I exult in the God of strength who makes me walk on high places—the God in whom I trust now more than ever before with a deeper and more mature faith.

Job's Example

About 25 years before Ben died, I was visiting a church in Garden Grove, California. It had a huge, beautiful garden filled with various pieces of art and statutes. One was a statue of a man called Job. The story goes that Job was a faithful man who trusted his Creator very faithfully. Calamity destroyed his possessions and family. Only Job and his wife were spared. We are told evil was not granted permission to destroy them, though for inexplicable and seemingly unfair reasons evil was permitted to destroy *all* else. At one point we read about the advice given to Job by his wife who said. "Why don't you curse your God and leave him who allowed this to happen to us." (paraphrased)

Job responded with these words: "Though He may slay me, yet shall I trust." (Job 13:15)

Who exactly did the slaying is up for debate; I have observed endless debates among a considerable number of Christian and Jewish authors. In the end they seem to agree to disagree on the slaying part. They simply do not have God's own infinite knowledge of God.

Very few of these theologians and authors, schooled in either the Torah or New Testament, disagree about the value of a deep trust in our Source.

A Piece of Art

Recently while listening to sacred chanting, I noted a particular piece of art which was used as a screen saver accompanying the music. It was a magnificent sculpture of Mary, the mother of Jesus. She was depicted as holding the cute innocent little baby Jesus close to her on her lap. In the corner of one of her eyes I could see a huge teardrop. What *really* caused me to pause, was her heart, over the left side of her chest, with a dagger through it.

When one loses a child that is what happens. An innocent, previously healthy heart gets pierced, and you bleed... and bleed some more... Every cell in the body experiences ineffable pain secondary to this profound piercing.

I now know that I can bleed and die because of the dagger penetrating my heart; I can get bitter, lose hope, or choose the Voice of Love, day by day, as I journey with many others who also suffer—just like me-- along a path called grief. I can choose to walk and keep going, but always with a limp. My choice is to run and refuse to let weariness derail me. I mount up like an eagle, empowered by Spirit in Whom I trust.

I move forward daily. Never alone. Always trusting. Always sustained by others and sustained by Love. Aware of Presence. A Love worth trusting, rather than cursing, as Job's wife suggested. I do not know why a Benevolent God did not answer my prayers, but I know I can, like Habakkuk, trust and be joyful with the God of my salvation. The perfect peace which guards my trusting heart is not there because of endless hours of meditation and psychotherapy—important as that may be—but the ineffable peace is there by sheer Grace. But it is up to me to surrender. To give consent via exercising my free will to trust fully.

Perfect Peace of Mind

I never knew about a passage in Scripture where we are told that when we trust in the God of the Universe, we shall encounter perfect peace (Isaiah

26:3) and in Proverbs, a Hebrew book of Wisdom, we read "*Happy* is he who *trusts* in God." (Proverbs 16:20)

I explained in a previous chapter the value of rituals— how a regular pre-dawn spiritual practice sustained me over the years. One of my habits is to recite the Peace Prayer of Saint Francis at least once or twice a week.

This prayer reminds me that some days—even when I trust I am not alone— I may lack inner peace. Although I have decided to make peace my main goal regardless of what happens to me; although I make peace the end I seek the aim of my living, my purpose, and my function…there will be days when I may have to recite the prayer more than once. Not just for my own sake, but also for the sake of others who lack peace.

Perhaps it will be my patients who are appointed to meet and need me in the hours that lie ahead; perhaps it will be to minister to a parent who is worried about a sick child; perhaps it is a parent who also lost a child or worries about losing a child to mental illness.

At the time of this writing our world is not in a peaceful state. It is quite unsettled by climate angst, political turmoil and fear of future pandemics. These are strange times indeed.

These are tumultuous times exacerbated by a global pandemic which created lockdowns, death, uncertainty, and significant havoc on every continent. The unintended major negative consequences caused by well-meaning leaders abound.

I see it in my clinic daily—teens scarred by well-meaning public policies, enforced upon us in a hurry, and possibly without considering long-term consequences properly.

The prevailing trend seems to be less and less peace in an era of more and more uncertainty and accelerated constant change.

The Buddha talked about the inevitability of change. We should not be surprised when it happens. But the pace and magnitude of the many changes happening *all at once* may explain the proclivity toward less peace in most humans.

It is with this in mind that the Peace Prayer of St. Francis (Paraphrased below) enables me to pray:

- Lord make me an instrument of your peace.
- Let me sow love which always triumph over hatred.

- Where there is doubt may I bring faith.
- And where there is despair may I be an instrument of hope.
- May my light bring some illumination in darkness.
- And may I bring some degree of joy where sadness prevails.

These are the sincere concepts contained in the prayer which goes on to ask that we may not so much seek to be consoled as to console; that we must understand rather than seek to be understood and to love instead of asking to be loved. It is indeed a prayer consistent with what the Mystical Messiah taught when he said it is better to give than to receive. As *A Course in Miracles* teaches, it is in giving that we receive. It is also true that in pardoning that we are pardoned.

Be Still and Know…Just Be

As I finish writing this chapter, I am sitting next to a candle. Candles symbolize various enlightened truths. They may provide light, insight, hope, or warmth. The good news is that light always overwhelms darkness.

On the other corner of my desk is a bright halogen lamp which sheds a warm glow onto my journals. In the quiet, sacred space of my study, before the sun rises, the sound of my fountain pen, smoothly gliding over the pages of my journals often is the only sound I can hear.

As I watch the wet ink slowly dry, I am reminded that on my heart, etched in timeless truths, with indelible ink, it is written that I am loved by an Infinite Love who sustains me. God's language indeed is silence as Rumi wrote.

My light, the candles, and the sacred silence, lead me to contemplate. Although these sources of Light and insights serve me well, it is only possible *after* the halogen light is plugged in to an electrical source, and then its switch has to pressed to the on position first. Only by following these two key steps I can see what I want to write. A light plugged in, but switched off, remains dark. To trust means to be plugged in. To stay connected and aligned with my Source.

In other words, in me *already* are resources provided by Grace, but I have to humble do my part which then allows a veil to be removed; only after that can one see clearly.

Abiding daily through contemplation in The Presence, I have discovered that when I keep my sorrowful heart plugged firmly into the socket of a loving Source, I experience perfect peace. And the more I am plugged into the True Light (John 1:9), the greater my trust and peace of mind. In the book of Acts (17:28) we read that in Spirit we live, move, and have our whole being.

I thank James Finley who reminded me via his soulful writings on how to meditate on Psalm 46:10. This well-known Psalm says, "Be still and *know* that I am God." (Italics added)

Often, I end my own meditations every day the same way as Finley ends his by reciting these words slowly and contemplatively:

Be still and know that I am God.

Be still and know.

Be still.

Be.

"I have no idea" Said Merton

I credit one of the fathers in our second family, V, who shared with us that he always senses he is floating somewhere in the middle of a deep and massive ocean. There are stormy times when he can hardly stay afloat and then these storms are followed by calm moments. But he is always floating...adrift in the middle of a vast ocean of emptiness. V is describing the fact that many of us have no idea where we are going at times.

That is the bad news; the good news is that when he looks around, he sees he is not alone; the second family floats with him. He trusts us as we stick together.

Thomas Merton wrote eloquently about trust. I use his words in many of my morning meditations as I set out for my days, not knowing what the day may bring and having no idea where I am going on the grief journey, because, like all of us, I wish there were less uncertainty and more of an anchor-related stability; more predictability and less of a sense of helplessly floating on a deep ocean of pain.

Merton wrote:

> *My Lord, I have no idea where I am going. I do not see the road ahead of me. I cannot know for certain where it will end. Not do*

I really know myself, and the fact that I think I am following your will does not mean that I am actually doing so. But I believe that the desire to please you does in fact please you. And I know that if I do this you will lead me on the right road though I may know nothing about it. Therefore, I will trust you always. Though I may seem to be lost and in the shadow of death, I will not fear, for you are with me and you will never leave me to face my perils alone.

***

I cannot say that I am comfortable with the uncertainties related to why our children died and I cannot say that I am fine with the fact that there are no more clues. I cannot say that I have the faith to guarantee that I will always have faith. But like Merton, I have decided to unconditionally trust a Mind infinitely in love with *all* of my being and a Mind far wiser than my own infinite mind can ever grasp. Like Merton, I too have no idea, but... but I trust fully.

When I am disconnected from my Source, the creator of the cosmos, I am powerless. But being connected via a deep trust I soar like an eagle and endure without limits.

In trusting unconditionally, and in giving up all hope of ever finding all the answers to all my questions, I fully surrender and let go—no more clinging or grasping.

I shall eternally be grateful for Buddhist teachers who helped my mind to remain in an equanimous state in the midst of uncertainty. The result for me is I have an experiential knowing that my decision to trust thus far—almost four years later—continues to sustain me, moment by moment by moment by moment. Here and now.

Here in my meditation posture as I silently utter the words, "Be still and know that I am loved and not alone."

Be still and know that I am God.

Be still and know.

Be still.

Be.

25

Mystics

Seek by reading and you will find by meditating, cry in prayer and the door will be opened in contemplation.
—Saint John of the Cross

In this chapter I want to talk about a profound experience I had three years after my son's death. This experience dramatically changed the trajectory of how I have chosen to relate to the aftermath of such a sickening tragedy. The personal experiences I am about to share in this chapter has helped me *immensely* as I continue to learn what it means to go through the bereavement process. I have surrendered to the reality of experiencing that which no parent wants to experience; that which all parents fear; that which happened to me and my wife.

How is surrendering to my reality possible and why is it possible? To answer these questions and to talk more about where I have ended up for now, I have to explain the evolution of my spiritual practice. This evolution has been pivotal in this journey—a journey of grief, but also a journey of attending to the inner being. On this inner journey, mystically and unexpectedly, discoveries were made about Something bigger and wiser than any other being ever present in form or in spirit.

The Pastor who Surprised Me

For the past twenty years I have followed the wisdom of one particular pastor whose ministry at the time of this writing has extended over almost half a century. He passed the test of time with flying colors. This man is respected by a wide swath of the population, not only in North America, but also in many parts of the world where he has followers and supporters.

He wrote numerous books, but one in particular, is kept close by in my study. In order to protect his fine reputation, I prefer to not mention his name—or the name of his book which made it on the New York Times bestseller list. (Over the years, many of his books regularly were on the New York Times bestseller list.)

In this book, which is well-written and widely read, this influential man covered the topic of mystics and mysticism. He was –much to my surprise—*not* in his usual fine form. Instead of being his gentle and kind self, he made fun of mystics and called them "mistaken." Mistaken? Yes... mistaken mystics. After his failed attempt to be witty, he flew into a rant. The longer I read his writings, the more it dawned on me that he is not alone.

Many well-meaning people feel uneasy when they hear or read anything related to mysticism. In short, mysticism is often avoided, usually out of fear and *mostly because it can easily be misunderstood.*

There are many definitions of mysticism and to lump all mystics as "mistaken" seems rather prematurely judgmental. Ultimately, a universal definition of mysticism will remain elusive and incomplete. And I suspect, for *that* reason this evangelical pastor remains "ignorant" of the true and mature teachings of the ancient Christian Mystics. Or he deliberately made fun of mysticism because he fears it may be misconstrued.

When asked about mysticisms I can relate to the answer St. Augustine gave. To me mysticism is similar to Augustine's comments when he wrote in his book, *Confessions,* about the definition of time: "What then is time? I know well enough what it is, provided nobody asks me; but if I am asked what it is and try to explain, I am baffled." (23)

Serendipity

Many times, when guests visit me in my study, they marvel at all my books. There are indeed many books; these books reflect the past trajectories of my life. They are like good old friends watching over me from the shelves graced by their presence.

I have been asked many times over by various visitors, "Have you read all these books?" And my answer was always, "Yes, I have. I love reading because I have a beginner's mind and just as I exercise my body daily, I believe that reading is to the mind what exercise is to the body."

There was only one problem with my answer: I lied.

It was unintentional. I missed reading *one* particular book.

I ordered the book four years prior to Ben's passing. For reasons I cannot explain, I placed it with a pile of other books, still to be read, but I never got to it. Inadvertently it ended up on a shelf—untouched and unread.

Three years after Ben's death, perhaps coincidentally, possibly by Providence, but after a series of serendipitous events preceding that moment one morning in my study, my eyes landed on the book, *The Big Book of Christian Mysticism: The Essential Guide to Contemplative Spirituality.* (24)

All through my life I received thousands of hours of spiritual teachings by various ministers, pastors, priests, and rabbi's. Over many decades I made it a daily habit to attend to my inner being. *Never* did I receive *any* teachings over six decades on Mystical Christianity...until three years after Ben's death.

I opened *The Big Book of Christian Mysticism* and scanned some titles; I read the introduction; I read the conclusion; I read the endorsements. Then I sat down with my fountain pen and a blank sheet of paper and got led, by an infinitely wiser Mind than mine—a Force whose love toward me is beyond comprehension— into a brand-new chapter of my life.

That chapter has not yet ended; like good wine it keeps getting better over time. I have concluded that it is impossible to exhaust all the insights of the Christian Mystics. It is practical and useful—especially when they write about suffering, spiritual aridity, living in uncertain times and ultimately facing the inevitable end —we all will face death itself. It is one more example of being sustained by the Love of God. I have intentionally designed this book so that I could talk about what sustains me the best in this last chapter.

Mystics who Were not Mistaken

It is indeed possible that my son, like other depressed teens, may have been able to survive, but to understand why he did not, will forever be difficult to explain. It has caused me indescribable amounts of suffering which taught me much. Contemplating the possible reasons why Ben decided to leave has become wearisome beyond description.

St. John of the Cross, a Christian mystic, wrote a book *The Dark Night of the Soul.* It is a book which explains why suffering may indeed be worthwhile. Can suffering become a teacher? Is it possible to write about *conscious* suffering? (25)

The suffering of St. John of the Cross and one of his acquaintances, St. Teresa of Avila, lead to numerous writings which clearly show that Mystics are not mistaken as the well-meaning pastor claimed: they are indeed seekers of a deeper level of intimacy with a Force much greater than ourselves. When we access the ancient writings of Mystics, we see how they have left us some very useful clues. They are not mistaken at all.

Mystics have paid attention to their sufferings and the Force who loved them through it all. As Carolyn Myss observes in a foreword to a book, *Saint Teresa of Avila: Passionate Mystic,* there is a "Force much greater than us, governing this world of ours." (29)

I have heard the name of Mirabai Starr in other spiritual circles, but never read any of her works. When I discovered that this dear mother lost a fourteen-year-old daughter, Jenny, in a car accident in 2001, I *immediately* became interested in what she wrote when she discussed the death of a child. As others observed, when one reads Mirabai's books, her elegant writing makes prose flow like poetry.

The Heart's Darkest Descends

In Mirabai's book, *Saint Teresa of Avila: Passionate Mystic,* she writes, "Teresa became my refuge, my source of healing, the container that held me through my heart's darkest descends." When Mirabai visited this sixteenth century mystic's convent in Spain where Teresa did her own writing, she talks about how "my heart swelled, and my eyes filled."

I have been privileged to read a number of books written by Christian mystics. Reading their marvelous, deeply thoughtful works requires a measured approach. It is best to just sit down in solitude and patiently soak in their deathless presence. Over time we learn that grief is a cross we carry, but we do not have to carry it alone.

I am absolutely amazed that these books, written as far back as the 12th century by monks, friars, hermits, and contemplatives, and written as a result of experiencing both mental and physical suffering, are as relevant today as they were eight centuries ago. It is as if one looks for insights to ease the pain of mental anguish the same way one looks for a warm sweater or coat to provide protection against extreme cold. And the works of the mystics, thousands of years later, are still a perfect match for one's current needs. The God of the Universe faithfully *continues* to provide deep intimacy through their writings, and in Presence is fullness of joy.

Very often the teachings of mystics transcend religious dogma. In fact, many of these mystics were tortured by their own religious traditions. Female mystics like Teresa of Avila were particularly attacked by paternalistic church leaders of her era who subscribed to the notion that women are inferior and thus never to be allowed to teach *anything*.

I suppose even today this gender discrimination could be one of many reasons that churches continue to be non-resonant to some. Those who believe that all God's children are special, but that none of God's children are more special, are particularly disturbed by a church who favors men over women. Men are *not* more special than women and vice versa. At times religion sees it differently.

Even those who consider themselves not religious have benefitted from the writings of St. Teresa of Avila. Mystical writers mostly deal with their deep yearning to relate—with an unquenchable thirst-- to God in a more intimate way.

These Mystics became wisdom figures who continue to transcend time, and stir our hearts, because they suffered greatly and long ago found what I have found since Ben died: one is never alone.

We are mystically guided— even when there may be moments when it happens without our knowledge or consent. I call that Grace at work, for our good, behind the scenes.

As James Dillet Freeman wrote: "The light of God surrounds me; His love enfolds me. The power of God protects me. The presence of God watches over me." There is indeed a deathless Presence who continually watches over me.

Mystics, purified by their own suffering, embody the words in the poem by Aeschylus, I referenced in the preface of this book. (*He who learns must suffer. And even in our sleep pain that cannot forget falls drop by drop upon the heart, and in despair, against our will, comes wisdom by the awful grace of God.)*

Prior to my son's death I never even knew about the writings of Christian Mystics. The discovery of how they processed suffering and misfortune helped me discover wisdom I never knew existed before.

Finding Meaning Collectively

A relatively more modern-day mystic and Trappist monk, Thomas Merton (1915-1968), became known for elegantly and prolifically describing his thoughts and meditations about God and suffering. Merton authored over forty books and was considered one of the foremost spiritual thinkers of the twentieth century. One of his most famous books, first published in the year I was born (1956), is *Thoughts in Solitude*. This book, alongside *The Seven Storey Mountain* are among Merton's most enduring and popular works.

One of the Merton quotes summarizes the essence of my belief about life in general:

> *"Love is our true destiny. We do not find the meaning of life by ourselves alone—we find it with one another."* (26)

These words are embodied by the Wednesday Warrior group my wife and I belong to. This group indeed continues to provide a forum for the faint of heart, by being meaningfully together, interwoven in our collective grief, and discovering that each member's fidelity toward recovering from the loss of child also means we discover how love is our true destiny, and that we are indeed not alone.

It can be said that we conspire together. The word "conspire" stems from a Latin word which means "to breathe together." The breath is a symbol of the spirit. When our group connects on a soul level, we sense a Healing Energy at work.

I am sure Merton, a Catholic monk, who was considered to be unique among his peers in that he embraced parts of Eastern mysticism--mostly because he experienced what it means to find meaning together--would understand if I were to call my second family my "Sangha." (A Buddhist term for community)

Mystics are not mistaken. They have left us clues—timeless, wise clues.

Destined to be contemplative

I was born with a curious mind and the fact that my medical career required a constant deep level of consciousness in order to make the correct diagnosis and provide the ideal solution to my patient's problems, meant that I always had to remain open to current information. It is by being open that we learn and grow. Wise discernment, however, is *always* essential.

To me, ongoing learning did not relate to the mind only—it holistically also included the spiritual; the unseen; that which is beyond form; the part of me which some call "the true self" or the "higher self" or the "deeper I."

As I mentioned in a previous chapter, at the age of sixteen I made the decision to follow the examples and teachings of Christ, after encountering a spiritual awakening. Between age sixteen and the time of Ben's death, my life was relatively free from suffering. Observing the suffering of my patients caused me to become increasingly philosophical and contemplative.

I made it a habit to record my actions and thoughts in a contemplative manner-- all throughout my life. Many of my friends and particularly my best friend, my wife, told me "You *really, really* think too much!" At times, my contemplative nature exasperates this dear woman, who embodies patience with my proclivity of always wanting to know how a turtle ended up on a post. Who put it there? And why?

And then Ben died by suicide.

Needless to say, I relied on what I have learned over decades; I prayed to get answers; I journaled. My own handwritten notes, created by my various fountain pens filled with black ink, royal blue ink, and lavender purple ink, changed blank pages of many journals into pages and pages of thoughtful notes. My desire to make sense of this life directed me to journaling as often as I could. The writings came from the depths of my heart; it evoked numerous thoughts and feelings related to the big question many of us ask: What is the purpose of this all?

Life Got Worse at First and Then Better

Ben's death preceded the Covid-19 pandemic by three months. Following Ben's death one of my sons decided to use excessive amounts of alcohol to numb his own pain. My other son relapsed into a deep depression. My daughter who has a strong faith, did what she was supposed to do: be loyal to her husband and her own tradition of Christianity; she rarely talked about Ben; it was as if it did not happen; she never initiated any conversations on the topic of his passing.

My wife could not return to her work as a Family Physician. She lacked the energy to work again. Authorities forced us to stay at home and isolate. In the newspapers and on TV there was nothing but incessant sad, negative news. It was as if the pandemic became the *only* news on the whole planet. Unprecedented times were unleashed during a morbid, divisive, protracted two years. The words "never seen before" populated newspapers daily.

The years of 2020-2022 were unique and painful, not just for our family, but for millions across the globe. Examples of collective suffering abounded all around the globe. It caused me to engage in even deeper and more frequent contemplative sessions.

But then life pivoted.

A Free App Arrives Just in Time

Shortly after the WHO declared Covid-19 to be a global pandemic, in a serendipitous manner, I was offered free access to a meditation app on mindfulness. While we were still in the midst of global chaos it was, in retrospect, where seeds of deeper mindfulness were planted. I discovered what it meant to attend to the body, the breath, one's feelings, one's mind. I also discovered that Buddhist psychology offers a pathway which leads to the better management of suffering.

Little did I know at the time that it was to become a solid foundation—both mentally and spiritually. It was merely the dawn of discovering the path to peace. The results of contemplative living were progressively being shaped—similar to a fetus evolving in a mother's womb in miraculous ways and under Divine direction.

Because so often mindfulness relates to Eastern traditions and wisdoms, I progressively discovered the psychological teachings of the Buddha. Buddhist teachings, as expressed in the Sati Pattana Sutta state this:

> *Mindfulness is the direct path for the purification of beings, for surmounting sorrow and lamentation and the disappearance of Dukka (unsatisfactoriness) and discontent; for attaining the true way and for the realization of freedom (nirvana)*

Buddhists take refuge in the Dharma (teachings of the Buddha) and the sangha (their Dharma communities) They are experts at teaching us how to abide in contemplation.

I want to make it very clear that I do not subscribe to the *religious* teaching of Buddhism.

But Buddhist *psychology* resonates for many—myself included-- because it is so very practical. Religious teachings in Buddhism are no different from other religions: it requires believing in that which cannot be proven. Buddhists also seek to become more mindful, without considering the Source of the mind.

I often wonder of it is possible that if one does not believe in a God or Creator, then one may end up making a god out of the workings of the mind, while ignoring any possibility of any Source. And still, what I learned from Buddhists regarding managing one's mind, will forever be priceless to me.

Consider it Joy

For three years after Ben's passing, I thought about my part in dealing with this tragic loss in the most mature way possible. I determined to be there for my wife and family, even though it made absolutely no sense, I wanted to discover how it is possible to "buy" into the words in the opening chapter of the New Testament book of James:

> *"Consider it joy, when you encounter various trials, knowing that the testing of your faith produces endurance and let*

endurance have its perfect result, so that you may be perfect and complete, lacking in nothing." (James 1: 2-4)

I read these words many times and talked about the true meaning with friends who I sincerely trusted. Count it all joy when you suffer? Absurd... yet true, and hard to explain unless post traumatic *growth* is understood experientially.

Even *then* it is simply ineffable. Words fall short. Even authors who made millions of dollars by selling their masterpieces via Oprah or the New York Times bestseller lists, do not have the skill to "stitch" words together which may come close to explaining the mystery of how we can be experience joy as a result of suffering.

Today, as I type the words you are reading, I find myself next to a candle, surrounded by my many books, which over decades have become like good old friends. I am looking at a small statute of Christ Jesus, the Shepherd feeding sheep, I am filled with joy –not that my son died—but that the result of his death lead me to a deeper relationship with my God. My intimacy with Him has never been deeper. I have ancient Christian Mystical writers and saints to thank for that. They indeed left me many, many timeless clues.

And the trust that I shall meet Ben again and be eternally united with him excites me to no end. It brings me boundless joy to read these words spoken by Jesus: "He who believes in Me will live even if after dying." (John 11:25)

By Grace I discovered the writings of Mystics who lived more than 1,000 years ago; their wise words ring true centuries later; words which are the product of their own contemplations, guided by Spirit, and shared with us as guideposts for surmounting our own sorrow, pain, and confusion.

My Teacher, James Finley

James Finley, a thoughtful and wise author, deeply influenced over many decades by the teachings of the early Mystics, delivers a podcast "*Turning to the Mystics.*" Finley grew up in a home with an alcoholic, abusive father. He discovered the writings of Thomas Merton as a teenager and decided to join the monastery in Kentucky where Merton taught and lived. Finley later became a psychologist specializing in trauma recovery. His wife, a recovering alcoholic, died from dementia during the dawn of the Covid-19 pandemic and it is with this as background that I would like to share Jim's wisdom when he explained how he experiences Christian Mysticism.

It was not an accident that at *exactly* 4:44 AM one night, I woke up, spontaneously, bathed in peace in my warm comfortable bed. I switched on my phone and clicked the play button of Finley's podcast. I heard him share his own experience—the experience of learning from a monk who lived in the 12th century.

How it Works

Guigo II, a twelve-century monk and mystic, wrote a classic book, only 17 pages long, known as *The Ladder of Monks*. Guigo wrote:

> *"One day, when I was busy working with my hands, I began to think about our spiritual work and all at once four stages and spiritual exercise came into my mind: reading, meditation, prayer, and contemplation. These make a ladder for monks by which they are lifted up from earth to heaven. It has few rungs, yet its length is immense and wonderful, for its lower end rests upon the earth, but its top pierces the clouds and touches heavens secrets."* (28)

Jim Finley then responded to the above, after the death of his wife, by reading Psalm 23, then reading it again and again, then meditating on the words, then praying the words, and finally entering a state of deep contemplation which he calls, "wordlessly resting in the presence of God beyond words."

Mystics taught that when we read Scriptures, it is God speaking to us, and then when we meditate, it is time for us to answer God's question: "What do you think? I have spoken to you personally, now it is your time to talk to Me."

Jim had a question for God. If Jesus always taught "fear not," then why was He disturbed and upset when he prayed prior to his crucifixion in the garden of Gethsemane? The contradiction profoundly bothered Jim.

When an interviewer asked Finley about religious teachers who oversimplify the complexities of living by stating that "Whatever the problem may be, all we need to do is simply pray it away," he answered:

> *"There are things in life we cannot pray away. Like the pain I feel about my wife's death, sleeping alone every night, I cannot pray that away. I cannot pray my sadness away. But I can learn to pray in the midst of my sadness and learn to listen to it and see what it has to teach me about life, and love, and whatever. So, prayer is not a remedy for getting rid of difficult situations. It is a kind of graced clarity that allows us to be clear minded, and real, and open in the midst of our situations. It is a big difference."*

Not to be Afraid of Being Afraid

Jim then explained that in answering God when God asked him, "what do you think of My scriptures" he had his own question; a question which made him wonder: "Is it possible then that I do not understand what You mean by not being afraid? Do You mean that to not be afraid, You are encouraging me not to be afraid of being afraid? I know You are going to give me the strength to get through this as best I can, and I will get through this in one way or the other. Are You asking me to have peace in the midst of engaging in this unfolding, painful loss I am going through? And is it that inner peace is not dependent on the outcome because it is Your peace upon which everything depends? You were not protected from the crucifixion. You protect me from nothing, even as You unexplainably sustain me in all things."

After hearing Jim explain his own experiences so eloquently, and in poetic terms, I got up later and journaled this in my study, using bullets to make my insights stand out—one by one:

- *To not be afraid of being afraid.*
- *To trust that the Love of God, The Infinite Presence, sustains me every second of my life—regardless of circumstances.*
- *To not have unrealistic expectations.*
- *To avoid delusional thoughts.*
- *To not feel sorry for myself.*
- *To rest wordlessly in the presence of a God who loves me with an infinite love.*

To be able to deal with the loss of a child, and experience the above, is indeed what mystical experiences are all about. It is hard to put it in words. But it is a deep inner knowing that the Love of God indeed sustains me... minute by minute; every second of my brief journey in this incarnation. That unfailing love, which has no end, will forever remain my refuge, my strength, and a very Present Help in times of trouble.

I end this book with the words expressed by an ancient 12th century mystic who summarized in one sentence what I tried to say in this book:

"It is not what I did, but what God did for me and through me."

THE END

Conclusion

The book you just read is really a book I wrote mainly for myself to better understand how to navigate the pain of a sickening tragedy such as having a teen die by suicide. Given the ever-evolving nature of grief, a book like this can never be finally written. There will always be more insights to come at a future date. Being blessed with a beginner's mind, I have given my consent to always learn more and the God of the Universe has responded as my Teacher.

I have learned so much about mental resilience. I have seen up close how people who suffer similar losses can bond together, and collectively open their hearts on a journey called grief. I have heard Ram Dass say that this life is all about how we walk each other home, and how we perform, not mouth-to-mouth resuscitation, but *heart-to-heart resuscitation.*

Burying a child is all about the piercing of a heart. And yet, I have learned things about suffering I may never have known unless I, by fate, was asked to ascend a spiral staircase and experience the gradual recalibration of my heart.

Grief is like a spiral staircase. Father Thomas Keating, writing in his book *Open Mind, Open Heart,* introduced me to the metaphor of a staircase representing a life of growth, transformation, and purification (19). Father Keating writes, "You seem to be returning to the point from where you started, but in actual fact you are at a higher level."

I agree with Keating when he puts it this way: "People who can live peacefully in impossible situations will make great headway in the spiritual journey."

I continue to make Divine peace my only goal, the end I seek, the function and purpose I have determined to pursue. My fidelity to doing the inner work required to find peace has led me to a higher level along the spiral staircase.

Peace is all I desire. It is *already* inside me, waiting to be unveiled via my inner spiritual journey; always going deeper and deeper, day by day. To become less and less impacted by circumstances is what Zen teachers refer to as "equanimity."

We slowly adjust to our new realities. Most of us, at some point, learn to say yes to losses; we accept that it is so and cannot be otherwise. To wish that things be as they used to be in the past is delusional. Those who resist accepting the reality of a child who died, will continue to suffer. To furiously fight that which happened, instead of becoming more accepting, is unskillful.

Acceptance is never easy (5). Grief is messy. It's many vicissitudes have a habit to toss us around like waves in a huge ocean. We fall overboard in a dark night, in the middle of nowhere. We are adrift in the darkness, but never alone. Any person experiencing the pain of bereavement must choose if he or she will utter these words: "I let go and I say let it be."

The *Serenity Prayer* contains these words: "Accepting hardship as the pathway to peace." The key word is "accepting." If the prayer were called *The Acceptance Prayer,* rather than *The Serenity Prayer,* it would have worked just as well.

At some point, if we endure our mental marathons, we come to understand the truth as expressed by Viktor Frankl, a doctor, and a Holocaust survivor, when he observed, "What does not break you, makes you stronger."

We slowly learn not to force our lives to be other than what it is. The path to the finish line of radical acceptance is signposted by patience, the first virtue of a life marked by Love.

My hope is that the life I am living now—a life re-written after a tragic misfortune—may inspire readers to never feel alone; never be hopeless; never be defined or destroyed by tragedy, but instead be lifted higher and higher along the metaphorical spiral staircase and being developed day by day; moment-by-moment-by-moment.

May our already-vast-hearts become bigger and hold more wisdom and compassion, not just for ourselves, but also for the well-being of others.

We are sustained... much more than we may ever realize, or fully understand. Sustained by caring human beings and by the customized tools we cultivate to alleviate our suffering. Above all, we are indeed sustained by Love. A Plus Factor. A Force I choose to call God, or the G-d who Scripture's call "The Great I AM." We are never abandoned... even though it may not be always clear or believable.

Ten Givens

I conclude with what I call the ten givens of suffering:

1. Sickening tragedies and misfortunes can happen at any moment. Nobody is immune. Do not be surprised.
2. Reasons are rarely clear. Do not endlessly seek answers, but instead love much. As Teresa of Avila said, "Do whatever best awakens us to love."(29)
3. Listen to Mr. Rogers: Look for the helpers.
4. We all need a customized anchor when storms arrive. Deal with how you design your anchor ahead of time.
5. We are not the *only* ones who suffer. We can learn to use our suffering to help others with *their* suffering.
6. We do have *some* control, but it is limited. Serenity means to let go of the things in life we cannot control.
7. Scars will result. Make sure yours embody refined gold (as in the art of Kintsugi.)
8. Suffering has stages. Aspire to arrive at the ideal stage—the stage where suffering provides meaning and purpose (7).
9. Expect a roller-coaster ride for the rest of your life. Learn to patiently endure.
10. Your departed loved one did not die... but transitioned from form to formless. Make sure you carry him or her in your heart *wherever* you are. (Since Ben left this world not a *single* day has passed where I did not carry him in my heart—regardless of the time of day and my location on this beautiful earth we inhabit but for a while.)

***

Acknowledgements

In our immediate aftermath, following the loss of our dear teenaged son Ben, helpers arrived by the dozens. I saw how humans are innately good and kind. Considering the impact such a tragedy has on parent's mental and physical health, my deep gratitude goes out to Drs. Brent and Susan Kinnie, friends of ours and Dr. Kim Wilmot, my personal physician. These fine physicians embody the true meaning of the word Doctor.

A mom who lost a spouse a number of years prior to Ben's death, Corinna Reynolds, experienced her own grief. As a result, Corinna provided invaluable help to my wife, in terms of dealing with the shock of losing a loved one so abruptly. Corinna's stoicism may appear to be her style outwardly, but her *inner* self, her compassionate, loving heart, and love for Christ Jesus enabled her to be salt and light in our lives.

Pastor Len Zoeteman, the pastor who married us in 1990 and who continues three years later to encourage me with his weekly text messages, truly embodies what a compassionate, wise, sincere pastor should look like. Our regular meals will go on to provide many more spiritual insights. Pastor Len, you are indeed a pastor's pastor.

My coach, Alan Cohen, even before Ben died, taught me that "Nothing real can be threatened and nothing unreal exists. Herein lies the peace of God." Alan also introduced me to *The Healers Prayer.* When I think of Alan and how he continues to remember my story, our story, and The Story of being sustained by the Love of God, all I can say in return is: "And so it is."

The men in my men's group—who I cannot name because that is just the way they wanted it—know how they sustained me. To be salt and light together, is a pursuit which evokes only memories of love, joy, and peace. Iron indeed sharpens iron.

To my Jewish friend, one of Canada's foremost sleep doctors, I say "Rob you are a real Cohen." A mensch. Your resilience inspires many.

Another mensch, Dr. Allan Donsky, provided useful and thoughtful feedback when he reviewed this manuscript. Allan challenged my beliefs by calling me "preachy" after he read Part III. However, I reviewed the manuscript and tried my best to ensure that my writings simply reflect my own beliefs—rather than convincing or judging others who may read Part III. Allan's wisdom and understanding of what the Buddha meant by the right view, impacted many of the words you have been exposed to in this book. Allan said it well" "No word is final, and no word is complete."

Our grief counsellors, Megan and Tara always told the group of grieving parents how we inspired them. Although that may be true, it is undoubtedly true that we shall never forget any of our Zoom calls during the Covid-19 pandemic. The hope, kindness, and insights you shared were infectious—especially at a time when "infectious" may have then meant Covid-19, until proven otherwise.

As I wrote in the last chapter, the ancient wisdom contained in the writings of the early Christian Mystics continue to remind me to think less, to love much, and to have a higher level of consciousness regarding the Presence of the Infinite. I thank these mystics for their deathless presence.

I also extend my deepest gratitude to Father Richard Rohr who reminded me that Christ, embodied in Jesus, was not a Christian, and that Christ was not Jesus' last name. James Finley's poetic and wise words continue to stir my heart daily. His books are right next to me as I type these words.

Brother Lawrence taught me much about the Presence of God (32). This friar, who died in 1691, wrote well about "feeling the inner nudges to bring himself back to the mindful practice of the presence."

My spiritual teachers who have different faith traditions taught me much about wisdom and compassion. Rabbi Matusof as an influential leader in the local Jewish community, embodies a profound and sincere kindness. And Professor Jadavji said it very well when he wrote me during Ramadan to explain how much his faith means to him. He wrote: "There are so many similarities between the three Abrahamic religions."

To Nadia Larson, a brave mom who stepped forward and offered to help edit this book: You are one of my sisters in our Second Family. Our Wednesday Warriors appreciate your kind and thoughtful leadership.

My wife who was the first one to discover that Ben died will always be the most important human being who continues to walk right beside me. We were recipients of a delivery we prayed may never happen. We prayed for the improvement of Ben's depression. It never happened and Ben died. *Together* we shall continue to get through what we are going through. Corinne, your wisdom, and strength will always amaze me.

And finally, as I ended the chapter on the Mystics, I end with the acknowledgement of my Savior who told me, "because I live you will also live." Christ made all this possible when I write these words:

It is not what I did, but what Christ did for me and through me.

***

Appendices

1

What parents told grief counsellors after completing a six-week group counselling session.

Adjusting better to initial shock and disbelief
New insights
Fresh perspectives
Not feeling alone
More aware of emotions
Courage to face fears
Self compassion
Not feeling alone
Relating to suffering of others
Learning from the strength of others
More hope
Inspiration
Not ok, but managing better
Feeling more understood
More connected
Safe space

2

Things to be aware of, and things you can do / or shouldn't do with a parent who has lost their child:

- Don't broach the subject of the child's death casually. If you ask, be sincere and don't cut the conversation off short.

- If these are people you love or care for, don't be afraid to ask about their child or how they feel and are doing. Do so respectfully and listen. Many parents will want to talk about their child.

- Be aware that the loss of their child is about the only thing parents are thinking of for a very long time after the death. It may be a year, it may be two, it may be five, or even more, before they are able to talk or think about anything else in a significant way. During this time, they really don't care about anything else in any real way. This is a reason that their friends and others may not stick around.

- Don't ever say or suggest you understand how they feel. Unless you lose a child, you don't. You're not even close.

- Don't compare the loss of a child to the loss of a parent, friend, spouse or similar. They shouldn't be compared. Losing a child is in a league of its own.

- Losing a child is the most difficult thing a parent can go through. Losing a child to suicide adds layers of guilt, blame and complexity that any parent in this situation will struggle to navigate.

- Be aware that there likely will be significant changes in the lives of parent's that lose a child. Holidays and gatherings may never be the same. There is a good chance that some or many of the friends and people they spent time with prior to the death will no longer be part of their lives in a significant way.

—The above ideas were shared by my friend Stephen Penner, a father in our second family, whose daughter also lost her battle with chronic inner anguish.

3

Resources during the grief journey.

David Kessler

Online
https://Grief.com Help for grief because Love never dies

Books
Finding Meaning: The Sixth Stage of Grief by David Kessler; Simon and Schuster Inc, 2019

Megan Devine

Online
https://refugeingrief.com

Books
It's OK that you are not OK, by Megan Devine; Sounds True Inc, 2017

Rick Warren

https://griefshare.org
https://hope4mentalhealth.com

4

The Five things We Cannot Change

- Everything Changes and Ends
- Things do not always go according to plans
- Life is not always Fair
- Pain is part of Life
- People are not loving and loyal all the time.

Sourced from David Richo; *The Five Things We Cannot Change... and the Happiness We Find by Embracing Them*
Shambhala Publications, 2005

Bibliography

1. Foundation for Inner Peace; *A Course in Miracles* Third Edition, 2007
2. Scott Peck: *The Road Less Travelled;* Simon and Schuster,1978
3. Kahlil Gibran; *The Prophet*; Pan Books Ltd; 1980 William Heineman Ltd.
4. Simon Jacobson, *Toward a Meaningful Life*; Harper Collins 1995
5. Tara Brach; *Radical Acceptance;* Published by Bantam Books; Random House December 2004.
6. Ram Dass; *Being Ram Dass;* Sounds True, 2021
7. David Kessler; *Finding Meaning*; Simon and Schuster Inc, 2019
8. Megan Devine; *It's OK That You Are Not OK*; Sounds True Inc, 2017
9. Richard Rohr: *Universal Christ;* Convergent Books, 2019
10. Richard Rohr; *Everything Belongs;* Crossroads, 2003Pengiun Press, 2008
11. Dhammapada: Translated by Eknath Easwaran, 1986, Nilgiri Press
12. Michael Pollan: *In Defense of Food;* Penguin Press, 2008
13. *Cloud of Unknowing*; Image Books; Random House 1973
14. Dr. Gerry Jampolsky MD; *Love is the Answer;* Penguin Random House, 1991
15. James Finley; *Christian Meditation;* Harper Collins, 2005
16. Jon Kabat-Zinn; *Wherever You Go, There You Are;* Hachette Books, December 2014
17. Joseph Goldstein: *Mindfulness;* Sounds True, 2013
18. Richard Rohr: *Naked Now;* Crossroad Publishing, 2009
19. Thomas Keating, *Open Heart, Open Mind*; Bloomsbury Continuum, 2019
20. Rick Warren; *The Purpose Driven Life*; Zondervan 2004
21. C.S. Lewis: *The Problem with Pain*; Harper San Francisco 1940
22. Alan Cohen; *Mystical Messiah;* Alan Cohen Publications, 2022
23. *Confessions of St. Agustine*; New City Press 1997
24. Carl McColman; *Big Book of Christian Mysticism*: Hampton Roads 2010

25. St. John of the Cross: *Dark Night of the Soul;* Amazon.ca; copyright2015
26. Thomas Merton; *Thoughts in Solitude:* Farrar, Straus and Giroux, 1999
27. Thomas Merton; *Seven Story Mountain;* Harcourt Inc, 1948.
28. Guigo II; Ladder of Monks; Doubleday & Company, 1979
29. Mirabai Starr, *St. Teresa of Avila. Passionate Mystic*: Sounds True Inc, 2007
30. Norman Vincent Peale, *The Power of Positive Thinking*; Prentice Hall, 1952
31. Dalai Lama and Desmond Tutu, with Douglas Abrams; *The Book of Joy*; Viking Penguin Canada, 2016
32. Brother Lawrence, *Practice of Presence* translated by Carmen Acevedo Butcher; Broadleaf Books 2022
33. Thomas A Kempis, *The Imitation of Christ*; Fontana Books, 1963

Benjamin Joshua Nieman
May 23, 2003 – January 1, 2020

Printed in the United States
by Baker & Taylor Publisher Services